“Errol Martens’ book is written in the cadence of his speaking, a firsthand mission adventure story full of faith, wry humor, and mission wisdom. As much as this is Errol’s story, it is also a moving testimony for alliances, partnerships, collaboration, and cross-cultural learning from each other. Missions and missionaries are always a work in progress, while the kingdom of God emerges in another culture and makes a profound difference in all areas of life.”

Paul Martinson

senior YWAM elder and teacher in YWAM Canada

OUT OF THE ICE

The healing power of Christ in Greenland

ERROL MARTENS

YWAM Publishing
Seattle, Washington

YWAM Publishing is the publishing ministry of Youth With A Mission (YWAM), an international missionary organization of Christians from many denominations dedicated to presenting Jesus Christ to this generation. To this end, YWAM has focused its efforts in three main areas: (1) training and equipping believers for their part in fulfilling the Great Commission (Matthew 28:19), (2) personal evangelism, and (3) mercy ministry (medical and relief work).

Some names and identifying details have been changed to protect the privacy of individuals.

For a free catalog of books and materials, call (425) 771-1153 or (800) 922-2143. Visit us online at www.ywampublishing.com.

All scripture quotations are taken from the KJV unless otherwise noted.

Out of the Ice: The Healing Power of Christ in Greenland

Published by YWAM Publishing
a ministry of Youth With A Mission
P.O. Box 55787, Seattle, WA 98155-0787

Library of Congress Cataloging-in-Publication Data — Pending

ISBN 978-1-64836-117-3 (paperback)

First printing 2023

Printed in the United States of America

International Adventures

Adventures in Naked Faith

Against All Odds

Bring Your Eyes and See

Cell 58

A Cry from the Streets

Dayuma

Living on the Devil's Doorstep

The Man with the Bird on His Head

The Narrow Road

Taking On Giants

Taking the High Places

Tomorrow You Die

Torches of Joy

Totally Surrounded

Walking Miracle

A Way Beyond Death

Contents

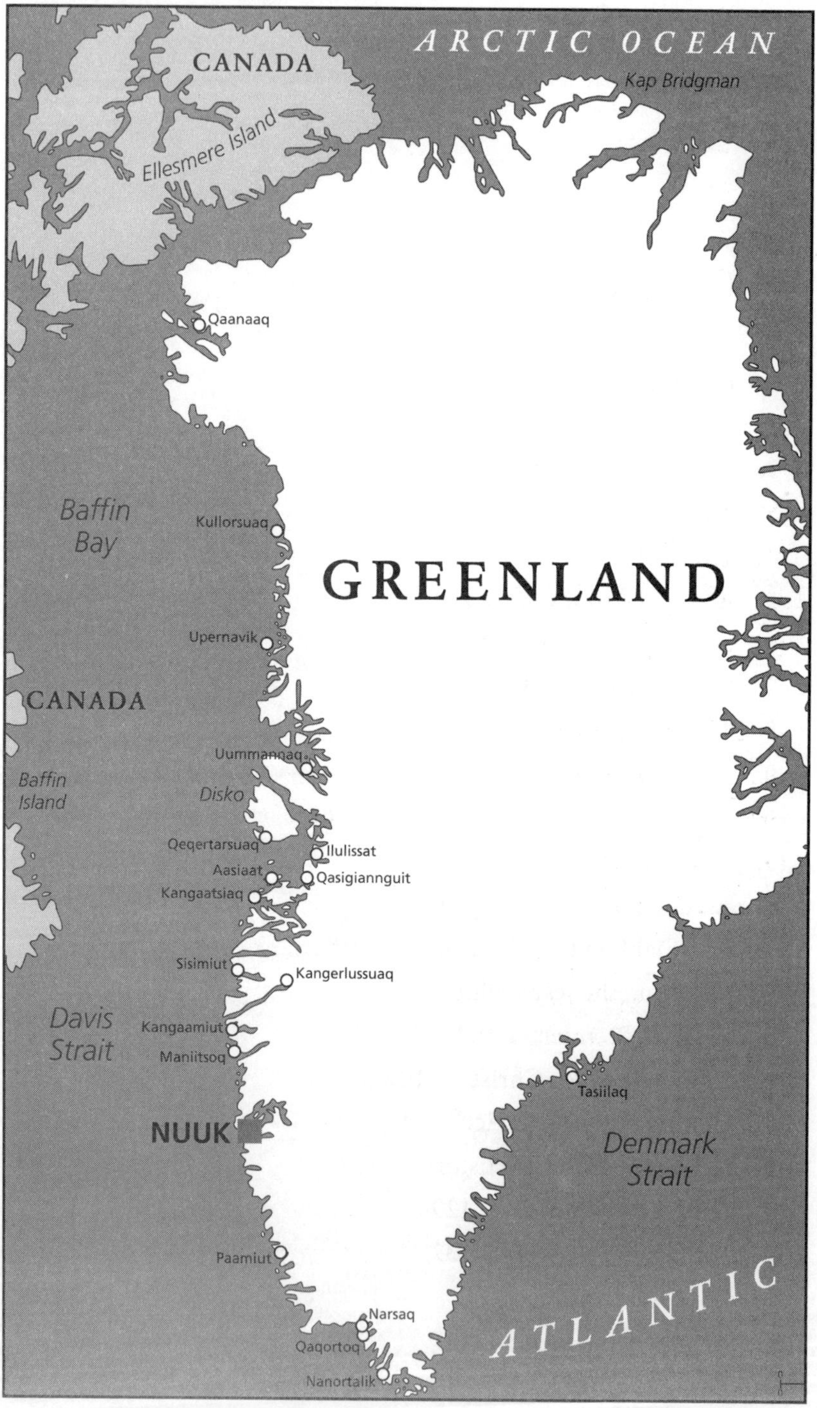
ARCTIC OCEAN
CANADA
Kap Bridgman
Ellesmere Island
Qaanaaq
Baffin Bay
Kullorsuaq
GREENLAND
Upernavik
CANADA
Uummannaq
Baffin Island
Disko
Qeqertarsuaq
Ilulissat
Aasiaat
Qasigiannguit
Kangaatsiaq
Sisimiut
Kangerlussuaq
Davis Strait
Kangaamiut
Maniitsoq
Tasiilaq
NUUK
Denmark Strait
Paamiut
ATLANTIC
Narsaq
Qaqortoq
Nanortalik

Introduction

IT DOESN'T TAKE much time for most people to think of a time in their lives where they became stuck in some way. If not stuck in a physical situation, then stuck in an emotional trap of hopelessness or even addiction.

I was once visiting a missionary in South Greenland. He told me about the time he was on board a passenger ship that became completely stuck in the ice.

Another time, I was hiking alone on a mountain in Canada. The trail became increasingly steep until I was climbing straight up and could go no higher. I carefully and slowly turned around to lean my back against the mountain face and was instantly gripped by fear. All I could see was empty air.

For over a decade I have had the privilege of sitting one-on-one with hundreds of individuals from many nations who felt trapped in emotional darkness.

One young man told me his story and then said, "I met my childhood abuser on the street the other day and beat him up. What do I do with this anger?" It didn't matter which town, which town hall, which church, which ministry center, or which nation we came to with our Healing the Heart course, we heard similar stories of desperation. Thankfully, by the time the course was completed at the end of the week, we heard very different stories. Stories of deliverance.

What happened to me on that mountain? I finally decided to let myself slide until my feet hit a ledge and I was on my way. And that ship the missionary was on? After three long weeks the ice shifted and the vessel was able to sail on.

Throughout this book I'm sharing many stories within a larger story. The overall theme is breakthrough and deliverance. Each challenging situation is unique, and therefore each solution is usually different. I believe you will be encouraged as you observe life-giving truths, values, and principals based in God's Word—all leading to wonderful outcomes.

I begin with my own "stuck in the ice" story, but I'm not alone.

Chapter 1

Peril on an Icy Sea

SAILING THE RUGGED coast of Greenland is not for the faint of heart, even on calm June days like this one. This remote Arctic country—the largest island in the world—is covered by a giant icecap, more than a mile thick in places. There are only thirteen towns and fifty-nine villages in all of Greenland. They are widely scattered along its 27,000-mile coastline, with no roads between them.

The hot coffee in my mug was swaying with the rolling ocean waves and also warming my hands. I steadied myself against the old door frame of the wheelhouse. Sven-Olov Åsblom had one hand resting on the large wooden steering wheel, a black captain's cap perched on his reddish-blonde hair. He seemed like a man born to be a Greenland sea captain. His ruddy features, powerful arms, and adventurous spirit were like those of the great Viking explorer Erik the Red. This son of Swedish missionaries was as kind and caring as he was tough. I was so glad he was piloting our group of Youth With A Mission (YWAM) students and staff through these brutally cold, dangerous waters of southwest Greenland.

There were sixteen of us on board, including my seven-year-old daughter, Tanya. At 32, I was the oldest one on this 46-foot wooden mission boat, *Evangelisten*.

Just a year earlier, Loren Cunningham, Sven and I had been sitting on the *Evangelisten* in Nuuk Harbour with YWAM's founder, discussing the idea of launching the first-ever Discipleship Training School (DTS) in Greenland. Sven's partnership helped make that dream a reality. We'd just completed the school's twelve-week lecture phase in Sisimiut at the mission facility, pioneered by his parents on the rocky west coast of Greenland, thirty-one miles (50 km) inside the Arctic Circle.

"Divine Guidance" is one of our mission's strong values, and in preparation for the evangelistic outreach that follows a DTS, we had everyone listen for an impression from God as to which direction we should travel. We were unanimous. It was South.

We left from Nuuk, arriving in the historic fishing village of Paamiut by early morning after Sven had captained the boat all night. We took a quick break to stretch our legs while exploring the area, but we were back on board by noon, heading south. As we sailed out of Paamiut the sky was blue. The air was calm, and brilliant icebergs of all shapes and sizes sparkled in the sunlight.

"The students are so excited," I said to Sven. "This is a grand adventure for them."

"Have everyone keep praying. These are dangerous waters. The ice is crowding in on us and it could get bad real fast," he replied.

"It looks like a perfect day to me."

"Yah sure, but I've lived in Greenland all my life. I see many good days go bad."

Sven's singsong-Swedish accent made me laugh. He is one of the most entertaining guys I've ever met and can make humor out of tense situations. Just then, a small speed boat appeared alongside our vessel with two Greenlandic men aboard. "We're turning back to Paamiut," they shouted. "Too much ice!" A new look of concern darkened Sven's face.

As evening neared, the waters of the Labrador Sea became choppy, ice floes dotting the seascape. We pressed on, but Sven began looking for a sheltered cove where we could spend the night. Meanwhile, our cook prepared a meal for the team, and Dave Skene, my co-leader, called us together for prayer. By the time Sven had anchored in calm water behind some barren islands, we were all weary and eager for sleep.

The bunks under the foredeck of the *Evangelisten* were all occupied, so Dave and I and my daughter Tanya slept on the narrow benches around the dining table. After thirty hours of continuous travel, we had no trouble dozing off.

The next thing I heard was Dave's voice. I opened my eyes to see him standing over me with a cup of coffee in hand.

"Come outside and look, Errol. A lot of ice moved in overnight."

The frigid air felt refreshing the moment I stepped onto the deck, but what I saw at sea stunned me, "Unbelievable!" was all I could say.

Soon Sven and the others were up. They stood silently staring. One of our Greenlandic students nimbly climbed up the mast and shouted something that sounded like "I think we have a problem!"

The great chunks of ice we'd seen the day before had multiplied into what looked like an army of giants blocking our way. At this point, we couldn't see if there was open water beyond the islands.

"Let's climb up there and see what we are in for." Sven said, pointing to a jagged, windswept mountain near the shore. He soon launched a skiff alongside the *Evangelisten*, and several of us got in and pushed our way through the ice floes to shore. When we climbed high enough to get a bird's-eye view of the ocean, the grim faces around me told me without words that our vessel was trapped. We saw no open water.

If we tried hiking to the nearest village north or south along this rugged coastline, we'd be blocked by icecap-fed fjords. These long and deep inlets are one reason there are no roads connecting Greenland towns. If we tried hiking east, we'd have to cross a range of mountains and cover 400 miles (643 km) of glaciers to reach the town of Tasiilaq, all the while trying to avoid slipping into an invisible crevice and icy grave.

My mind was racing. *Those ice floes may not move for weeks! We don't have much food and water on board. What if our supplies run out before the ice moves? This ice can easily crush a stationary wooden boat. Is our outreach over before it has even begun? And how will the students respond to this dire news?*

If the others had these kinds of thoughts as we made our way back down the mountainside, they didn't voice them—and it was a good thing. We'd need all the positive, victorious words of faith we could muster.

Back on the boat, I called everyone together.

"We could see no open water from the mountain," I said through an interpreter. "We were scheduled to arrive in Narsaq by tomorrow, but now we have no idea how long it will take." Everyone stood there looking at each other with an occasional glance out to sea.

"Before leaving on this outreach," I continued, "we all prayed and asked God which part of Greenland we should focus on, and it's the direction we are now heading. We have an impossible looking obstacle. The question is not *Why?* The question is *How will we respond?* And so I'm asking: How does a believer respond?"

"They pray!" shouted one of our vibrant Greenlandic students.

"Okay, let's join hands right now." It was heartwarming to hear one prayer of faith after another offered up from around the group.

"Now, let's quiet our hearts," Dave led out, "and listen for any impression the Lord may give us for how to proceed." The air was still except for the occasional thud of ice rubbing against the wooden hull of the boat. After a few moments of silence Dave continued, "Please, share any impressions you receive."

"I have the impression we are to press on," Scott declared, with Rutt, our Norwegian student translating. Rutt, like Sven, had been raised in Greenland to missionary parents and spoke fluent Greenlandic.

"I also thought of the Children of Israel, who were in a situation similar to what we are now in," Scott continued. "The whole nation was enroute to the Promised Land, but they were blocked by the Jordan River, which was at flood stage and overflowing its banks. Getting all their men, women, children, animals, and supplies across that deep and fast-moving water seemed impossible. God basically said, 'Just do what I say and you'll get across. Now get packed up and ready to go.' Then God told the priests who were carrying the Ark of the Covenant to start wading into the water. As soon as they did, the water upstream stopped flowing and they got across. Faith based on the Word of the Lord requires a correlating action."

After Scott's word, we all knew what we needed to do, and Sven was in full agreement. We assembled ourselves for departure. Gently easing the bow of the diesel-powered vessel against a heavy ice floe, Sven gradually increased power with water churning up like a disturbed sea creature. But the thick Arctic ice was stubborn. The boat was going nowhere.

Stuck in the ice
From a high perch on the Evangelisten a DTS student searchs for a way.

Chapter 2

Pain and Redemption

THIS WASN'T THE first time in my life I'd faced a seemingly impassable barrier. The internal wall of discouragement I felt as a child and teenager often had felt even more hopeless than confronting a wall of ice floes.

Though I grew up in a stable Christian home with good parents and a delightful younger sister, I was a shy and skinny kid who often retreated to the outdoors. When I was 11 years old, we moved from Calgary to Burnaby, a suburb of Vancouver, British Columbia. I quickly discovered the thrills of the forest and creek nearby. I never felt alone in the wilderness, but I often felt alone around other kids.

One day when I was out delivering newspapers, a gang of boys started pelting me with dirt clods. As the hard clumps bounced off my jacket, I felt shamed. In my anger, I grabbed a smaller boy standing nearby, threw him to the ground, and punched him in the face. Now he was the one getting shamed. The problem was he had a big brother.

The next day as I walked onto the school grounds the brother grabbed me from behind. While I was immobilized, the boy I'd punched the day before began kicking and punching me. The worst part was the crowd of kids gathering around to watch. I was shamed ten-times more than I had been the day before. I felt picked on throughout my childhood, and this event increased my contempt toward others. Unless someone I met was immediately friendly, I believed they were against me.

Not only did I find it easy to reject others, I didn't like myself either. I believed the lie that I was not likeable, talented, or smart. I got poor grades at school, started shoplifting, and was headed down a misguided path. One time, a teenage friend offered me drugs. Thankfully, his invitation scared me. When I refused, he threw his stash into the bushes.

I thought I was a Christian because I attended church with my family. I participated in youth group meetings at church and even joined other youth for large evangelistic rallies. I asked Jesus to save me, but because there was no repentance, it didn't make any difference in my thoughts, words, behavior, or feelings.

At age 16, I discovered bodybuilding. At that time I was a meager 129 pounds and felt the need to "bulk up." It seemed I was getting left behind in physical size on the school ground and fighting was no longer a safe option for venting anger.

After six months of dedicated weight training I'd gained a whopping eight pounds of muscle, not bad for a fine-boned skinny kid. Even more impressive was the strength I had gained. People were starting to notice my appearance changing, and it felt good. The training gave me new goals in life, and I was passionate about getting bigger and stronger. There was just one problem: weight training did not address the restlessness of my heart. There was still a nagging discontent, a sense that there must be more to life.

That's why, on a crisp fall evening in 1970, while I was alone in my bedroom, I cried out to God: "If you exist, show me yourself once and for all, or I might as well forget the Christian thing altogether!" Tears were streaming down my cheeks. In my mind's eye, Jesus was frowning at me. It seemed to me that *everyone* was frowning at me in those days! But Jesus was about to change that perception.

The next evening our church hosted a youth rally and the speaker, an author named Josh McDowell, grabbed my attention with his shockingly honest testimony. The feelings of pain and shame he'd experienced as a boy were even more intense than mine. He said he hated his alcoholic father and almost murdered him. His emotional foundation had been rage. But instead of asking, "God, if you exist, show me!" like I did, the speaker said he made it his passion while at university to prove God *didn't* exist. After years of extensive research, he found the evidence for God's existence, the resurrection of Jesus Christ, and the validity of the Bible to be so overwhelming, he became a believer. He subsequently wrote a book on his findings called *Evidence That Demands a Verdict*.

What spoke even more directly to my heart that weekend was a little blue booklet McDowell was making available at the rally. It was called, *Have You Made the Wonderful Discovery of the Spirit-Filled Life?* by Dr. Bill Bright, founder of a ministry called Campus Crusade for Christ, now called CRU[1].

I read in the booklet that a person who thinks he is a Christian but struggles with issues like jealousy, guilt, worry, lust, discouragement, criticism, frustration, aimlessness, fear, and prayerlessness has probably not allowed Jesus to be Lord, and even more, might not be a real believer at all.

"Wow," I thought to myself. "All this describes me exactly!" The little blue booklet went on to say, "The way to experience the fruit of the Spirit; like love, joy, and peace… is to make Jesus Lord, and invite Him to 'sit on the throne of your heart.'" In other words, yield to His will, His wisdom, and His Holy Spirit.

I made that choice, and the peace of God flooded my heart. Over the coming months my love for God and my faith grew, the Bible became life to me, and restlessness and boredom were gone. I was about to be launched into a life of adventure I'd never even imagined.

1 Known as *Power to Change* in Canada

Chapter 3

Overseas Adventures

One evening I went with some friends to a large church in Vancouver BC, to hear a special speaker well-known in Christian circles for his daring work smuggling Bibles into communist countries. I was inspired by his message, but even more so by a man who followed him to the pulpit.

Don Stephens, a young American leader of YWAM, was burning with vision. He declared, "Next year in August, the 1972 Olympic Games will be held in Munich, Germany. Thousands will be there from many nations, including many from closed countries. It will be an opportunity to reach the world in one city. I'm calling on hundreds of young people to come to Germany to present the gospel during the Olympic Games. If you are interested, stand to your feet!"

I didn't stand at that moment, but I did stay after the service, along with many others, to fill out a response form. When I handed it to Don, he looked me in the eye and said, "Maybe we'll see you there, huh?" Maybe. At that point, I had no idea.

A couple of months later, I enrolled at Briercrest Bible Institute in Saskatchewan Canada. I enjoyed campus life, but I sensed God had something more for me. My thoughts kept returning to Don's invitation to Munich. One evening alone in my dorm room I prayed, "God, you are so great, you must have more for me than what I've lived so far!"

In Matthew 7:7, Jesus promises, "Seek, and you will find; knock, and it will be opened to you." I found what I was searching for that next August in Munich. The YWAM Olympic Games Outreach exposed me to a level of Bible teaching, passion for God, faith, and world evangelism that I'd never witnessed before. My prayer for experiencing more of God was answered powerfully, and it would only get more amazing.

Hundreds of Christian young people responded to the call to Munich, and their passion for Jesus touched the nations. Toward the end of the three-week outreach, various YWAM leaders stood up to give their own invitations for more overseas evangelism. One said, "Come and join the outreach to East Africa." Immediately my heart leapt. I'd always wanted to see Africa—mainly because of Tarzan, my childhood hero! But now I prayed, "Lord if you want me to go to Africa for your glory, I will."

My love for Jesus eclipsed my love for Tarzan. Jesus was real! Jesus changed lives! And Jesus said, "GO!" (Matthew 28:19–20). So I did.

Our team arrived in Nairobi at night, so I couldn't see much on our drive to the Salvation Army building where we'd be staying. The next morning, I stepped outside the front gate. Soon, I was engulfed in people, all of them black. It was my first culture shock. Coming from mostly white Western Canada, I'd never seen that many black people in my whole life, and I didn't have any black friends. At the end of the street was an open market. There were men building beds out of wood and strips of rubber cut from old car tires. Other stalls had fruits and vegetables and raw meat buzzing with flies.

The second night there, we were awakened by a horrific scream. I jumped out of bed to see what was happening. The night watchman caught three thieves trying to get in the back door and screamed to scare them off. He carried a large machete while on duty, so that probably frightened the intruders more than the scream. We were all safe but unnerved by this introduction to Africa.

In Nairobi, we were formed into four teams. One team to Zambia, one to Tanzania, one to Ethiopia, and one to stay in Kenya. To my surprise, they chose me as leader for the Kenyan team. I was only 19 years old. After prayer, I was given a lesson on leadership: "Errol, always stay one step ahead of your team." And that was it! I soon came to love this about YWAM, how easily, yet prayerfully, they released young men and women into leadership. Things can go a little haywire when leadership is entrusted to young people, but it can also be a great way to develop leaders. Years later, Loren Cunningham said to me, "Releasing youth is a risk, but once you stop releasing, your mission starts to die."

A 24-year-old Swedish woman was put in charge of all 23 participants who'd come from Munich. She'd been in Africa before and had the respect of other leaders there. I soon came to appreciate her as an older sister in the faith. Up until that point I'd never been chosen to lead anything in my life. But when asked to lead the Kenya team, something stirred inside me. It was life-giving.

We were there to tell people about Jesus. Our team spoke in school classrooms, churches, and open-air settings wherever we could gather a crowd. We moved on from Nairobi to Mombasa, north to Tana River, over to Lamu Island, and then south down a dusty road into Tanzania.

Early on our team connected with a 25-year-old Masai evangelist who was a great preacher with an engaging personality. His presence was such a valuable contribution and support to our young team. Everywhere we went, we preached, gave our testimonies, handed out gospel tracts, and visited missionaries and African pastors.

A bite-size part of a message I heard from our Masai brother has stuck with me for decades:

"and Jonah ran away from the Lord and went *down* to Joppa, then he went *down* to the harbor, then he got *down* into a boat, then he went *down* below the deck, then he went *down* into a deep sleep (to avoid his conscience?), then he was thrown overboard and went *down* into the sea, then he went *down* into the belly of the fish! And that's what happens when we run from God! Our lives will go down, down, down until we repent. Jonah spent three days in that fish's smelly belly before he repented and got thrown up onto a beach!"

As we drove through the countryside, we saw giraffes, elephants, baboons, and monkeys, but the closest I got to Tarzan was me hanging on a vine for a picture.

After six months in Africa, I was starting to feel at home. I'd come to love the African people and African food like *ugali*. Even my feet were brown and dusty, tucked into the flip-flops I'd been wearing almost exclusively all those months. They'd also doubled as a handy cockroach swatter when needed.

That Kenya outreach changed me in so many ways. I was now more on fire for God and missions than ever, and I'd come to deeply appreciate another culture and people. I didn't want to leave. I loved East Africa. However, my visa expired, and when I handed my passport over to an official in hopes of an extension, I watched instead as he wrote, "EXIT."

As the airplane roared down the runway, images of Africa, my team, the people, and my experiences with God flashed before my eyes. I turned my head away from the man next to me and burst into tears.

Chapter 4

Times of Preparation

THOUGH IT WAS hard to leave Africa, I enjoyed sharing about my adventures with my parents and my home church. It was also good to be home because I had suffered through a bout of malaria and needed rest. I also needed fresh guidance. I wanted to continue in missions work but had no clear direction about my future.

I've learned that God uses seemingly directionless "wilderness" times to prepare us for future adventures in faith. Sometimes the first step is discovering what *not* to do. A few weeks after returning from Africa, I heard that Joy Dawson would be teaching right in my city of Burnaby, BC. This spiritually passionate New Zealand woman had been one of the main Bible teachers at the Munich Games outreach. Her teaching was inspiring, clear, thorough, and practical. She taught on *How to Hear God's Voice and Receive Divine Guidance*. I took careful notes in anticipation of joining a new YWAM ship ministry. It sounded exciting, but how could I know what would be right for me?

At one point, Joy exhorted us to resist predetermining how God should speak. "Be open even if it means randomly flipping the Bible open and pointing at a verse," she said. That method sounded crazy, but after spending time preparing my heart according to her scriptural teaching, I finally said, "Lord, if it is your will to speak to me by using this flip-open-the-Bible method, I am willing."

I opened my Bible, and slowly peered at the verse I had randomly selected. Sure enough, it contained the word "ship," and the context was negative. I was in awe. Then I remembered Joy quoting 2 Corinthians 13:1b "In the mouth of two or three witnesses shall every word be established." That's a good principle when it comes to important decisions. Perhaps she did not mean to continue using this "flip" method, but that's how I proceeded.

My heart was pounding as I prayed and opened the Bible. Again, my eyes landed right on a verse about a ship. It was a completely different verse and again, the context was trouble. I was feeling God's presence and peace so strongly that I did it a third time. I opened to a different verse, again with the same result. I received exactly what I'd asked for, verses containing the word ship with a negative or positive context, depending on whether God wanted me to join that ship ministry or not. His direction couldn't have been clearer.

With new confidence I dropped the idea. It was the right decision, as the ship ministry took an abrupt delay, and was not birthed until years later.

Instead, God took me in quite an unexpected direction—one that at first, I didn't recognize as important in preparing me for missions.

The nudge I kept feeling in my spirit was to get involved in a summer children's outreach. I didn't want to, but I dutifully called the office of Child Evangelism Fellowship (CEF) to see if they needed help. Hoping they would say no, I asked, "You don't need workers for this summer, do you?" The receptionist responded, "Oh yes, we do need workers! When can you join us?"

I signed up for the next CEF training session, and as soon as I walked in my heart sank. Our volunteer group had thirty girls and just two guys! *No wonder, this is not a guys' thing to do!* I thought. The training wasn't nearly as dynamic as what I'd had in Munich. It was all about presenting

Bible stories to kids. After the first day, I prayed, "Oh Lord, I feel out of place! After all, I've led an outreach team in Africa! Now you want me to do little kids clubs?" It was a severe blow to my pride, but I didn't quit.

One day in my morning quiet time, I began reading Isaiah chapter 45. Suddenly, the power of God's Word gave me the change in perspective I so needed. In Verse 2, the Lord says, "I will go before thee, and make the crooked places straight: I will break in pieces the gates of brass and cut in sunder the bars of iron." These words literally broke through my sour feelings and lifted me to a place of peace. As I continued reading the promise of Verse 3, my spirit was encouraged even more as the Lord continued His promise. "And I will give you the treasures of darkness, and hidden riches of secret places." To me this meant, "as the summer unfolds, treasures and riches await you." That was like a jolt of power to a weak battery.

And, sure enough that summer turned out to be another life changing experience. I loved traveling through British Columbia in my little red Volkswagen. And I related well with the kids! My ministry colleague and I worked in seven different towns. We led four clubs per day, two in the morning and two in the afternoon, in the back yards of willing hosts

The CEF program used simple storytelling methods communicating biblical truths in an engaging way. I loved the stories of Jesus and so did the kids. I later discovered this storytelling approach also worked well with adults. That summer fifty children expressed a desire to follow Jesus. I felt these children were the treasures God had spoken about.

God's promise from Isaiah 45 became a reality to me in so many ways. Instead of condemning me for my pride, the Lord gently encouraged me with his love, wisdom, and goodness. Jesus said, "Let the little children come to me and do not forbid them for such is the Kingdom of heaven." (Mark 10:14 NKJV) That summer, I came to see just how important children are to God.

In the fall God led me to enroll at Berean Bible College in Calgary, where He strengthened me with solid biblical training and surprised me with a relationship that would change the course of my life.

One classmate I noticed right away was a petite, slender woman with long black hair and a sweet, freckled face. Her name was Joyce, and

I discovered that she grew up on a farm in Alberta. Her background brought an immediate curiosity. In my youth, I loved visiting my relatives' farms in Saskatchewan, where both my parents were raised. When I was 17, I got to work on a farm for a whole summer and at harvest time. My grandmother once advised me, "Marry a farm girl."

I loved Joyce's spirited personality—a trait matched by her quick mind, quick responses, and quick decision-making. Somehow, I sensed these qualities were a good balance to my personality. Most importantly, she had a heart for God and for missions. As we got to know one another, I warned her, "Joyce if you stick with me you might end up in an African mud hut. I just want you to know that!" It didn't seem to faze her at all.

We often took walks together on a tree-lined street near the bible school. Joyce liked to walk even when it was raining. I asked her on one of our walks, "Why do you like walking in the rain?"

"I don't know. I've always loved the smell of the clean air and fresh earth after the spring rains. And I love a good prairie thunderstorm, too!"

God was still working on my heart, and in Joyce's too. I sensed it would take a lifetime to truly know one another, and we both were moving in that direction.

On one of our walks she asked, "When's your birthday?"

"New Years' Eve."

"Really? That's the same as my birthday too!"

"Wow! That's an amazing connection."

We also shared a YWAM connection. She had completed a School of Evangelism in Europe so she understood my passion for missions. Over time I came to believe Joyce was the right woman for me.

We married on September 3, 1978, in a beautiful ceremony at Bethel Baptist Church in Calgary, Alberta. Both sets of parents were there plus many friends and relatives. By the time we were married, I'd been pastoring a little country church just east of Calgary. Joyce joined me in the snug little manse next to the church on a half-acre of pastureland. I never expected to become a pastor, but I came to love those people.

At Berean Bible College, I was taught to preach using an expository rather than topical approach. The expository method goes book by book through the Bible, expounding on and applying the principles within each section. I loved that kind of teaching, but in January 1980, I decided to teach a four-part series on a topic near to my heart—Hearing the Voice of God. It included what I had learned from Joy Dawson, and I now had my own stories to tell. But little did I know, our biggest story to date was just around the corner!

Chapter 5

A Shield Around Us

ONE DAY MY young wife said to me, "Where should we go for our first vacation?"

I replied, "Why don't I practice what I've been teaching and ask God?" That afternoon I went into our bedroom, knelt beside the bed, and began preparing my heart to hear. I started by meditating on Proverbs 3:5–6. "Trust in the LORD with all thine heart; and lean not unto thine own understanding. In all thy ways acknowledge him, and he shall direct thy paths."

Then I used my imagination to stretch my faith and human boundaries. "Lord, if for this holiday time you want us to go to India or Russia or South America or just down the road to Rosebud, Alberta, we will go."

Before bed that night I turned to the next chapter in my Bible reading. It was Genesis 29:1, "Then Jacob went on his journey, and came into the land of the people of the east." These words stood out to me.

Just a few days earlier, Joyce and I had been listening to reports about the plight of Vietnamese boat people in Southeast Asia and about the bloody purges of Pol Pot's regime in Cambodia. Then, the next day I randomly opened *Time* magazine and viewed an ad for travel to Thailand. It seemed like everywhere I looked Asia hit me between the eyes.

After about three days Joyce asked, "So where are we going?"

I said, "I think I know."

"Well, tell me," she urged. I was tempted to tell her because I felt that familiar sense of peace, confidence, and excitement knowing I'd heard from God. Still, Joy Dawson had wisely taught to not be too quick in sharing guidance. God wants each of us to seek His direction and confirm together the guidance given.

"No, you find out for yourself," I said with a smile. Joyce walked down the hall to our bedroom. When she came out, she said, "Well, one thing I know, this will be a holiday with a purpose." How prophetic her words would turn out to be!

"Let's just give it a few more days and see if you receive the same direction," I replied.

There was a long pause, and then Joyce looked up at me and said, "We are going to Asia, aren't we?" I couldn't believe my ears! I wasn't expecting that so quickly.

In March 1980, we arrived in Hong Kong. We soon connected with YWAMers serving at Jubilee Camp, an old army barracks that was built to house 600 soldiers and now sheltered 6,000 Vietnamese refugees. Because of our connection with YWAM, we were able to enter the camp and see for ourselves the plight of these people who had risked all to flee the North Vietnamese invasion into the South. The experience made a deep impression on us.

While in Hong Kong, we stayed at the YMCA. It was no tourist destination, but it did house one special guest, T.C. "Tom" Cunningham, father of Loren Cunningham. One evening we decided to go up to his room and see if he was available to talk with us.

Tom greeted us with a smile as wide as his native Texas. This influential Assemblies of God pastor and missionary towered over us both, but immediately impressed us with his warmth, humility, and humor.

Soon he was telling us captivating missionary stories and talking about China.

"During the Cultural Revolution under Mao, the communists gathered up all the Bibles, piled them in town squares, and lit them on fire. Then they forced Bible believers to kneel around the fire very closely, until their faces were blistered from the heat. For decades, the country has been tightly closed to foreigners. Now the government is starting to allow tourists in. Some missionary organizations are taking advantage of this opportunity to bring in Bibles."

I replied, "We met a missionary here who told us he was involved in Bible smuggling. He said Christians in China are desperate for Bibles," I replied.

"Yes, Errol. They are."

The missionary we met through YWAM Hong Kong suggested Joyce and I go to Canton (now Guangzhou) on a three-day arranged tour and bring Bibles with us. He made it sound so easy, but it didn't feel like a very straightforward thing to do considering all the stories I'd read about persecution of Christians in communist countries. "Give us a couple of days to pray about it," I told him.

The next day I was resting on our bed and praying about the decision. A memory came to mind that seemed like the Lord speaking. "Remember when you asked me, 'Why are we going to Southeast Asia?' I spoke to you through the life of Jacob in the book of Genesis and said, 'When you get there, I'll tell you why I'm sending you.' "

This revelation clinched my decision. My response: "Yes, Lord, we will do it and trust you're with us."

* * *

The missionary, who looked like a professional football player, lugged three heavy suitcases packed with Chinese Bibles into our small hotel room. *It's a good thing I've done weight training,* I thought as I lifted each one. It wasn't so easy for Joyce though, so we decided we would take two bags between us. Still, there were at least 800 New Testaments as well as other very valuable Christian literature.

Our tour was organized by Joy Travel Service LTD, in Hong Kong. It included the journey to Canton, two nights in a hotel, all meals, a theater performance, visits to a commune, a silk factory, an ancestral temple, and the Kwangchow Museum.

We left from the Tai Kok Tsui Ferry Pier in Kowloon and were soon roaring up the Pearl River on a hydrofoil boat to Canton, seventy-five miles (120 km) north of Hong Kong. Chinese soldiers were patrolling the ancient dock as we arrived. "Don't be afraid," I whispered to Joyce, who was feeling very anxious. "God is with us."

The Red Army soldiers dressed in green uniforms with red stars on their caps looked intimidating, and to our alarm one of our heavy suitcases split open a crack as it was unloaded onto the dock. We could see the books inside! Amazingly, no one else seemed to notice. With pounding hearts, we made it through customs with no inspection of our contraband-laden luggage. Our two large suitcases were waiting for us at the hotel. Late that evening, after enjoying a multi-course Chinese meal and attending a show at the Friendship Theater, we were scheduled to deliver the Bibles to two couriers outside the hotel.

It was dark, and drizzling rain made this meeting feel even more like I was in a spy movie. Soon I noticed two men coming toward me from down the street. *Were these the couriers?*

No, they walked right past. The delivery time came and went with no contact. I returned to our room dejected.

"Joyce, no one came. What are we going to do with all these Bibles?" Even though it was way past the set time to meet she said, "Maybe they were just delayed! Anything could have happened! They might still come!"

Apprehensively, I took the elevator down the 22 floors and walked out into the murky darkness to wait again. It was well past midnight by the time I went back up. Joyce was sitting wide-eyed on the bed, tense from waiting so long.

"They just didn't come," I said. We were whispering now, thinking of all the possible bugs in the hotel built for foreigners in a country that had been under strict communist rule for thirty-one years. Joyce nodded, but I could feel her dismay as we went to bed.

We had no idea what to do next. There had been no instructions past delivering those Bibles on the first night of arrival. Before I turned off the light, I read Psalm 3, and the last verse was like a dramatic ending to a Beethoven concert. It said, "Salvation belongeth unto the Lord; thy blessing is upon thy people." I felt the Lord saying, "Those Bibles are going to get where they are intended!" With that assurance, I slept peacefully. I wish I had read that Psalm to Joyce. She tossed and turned all night.

All the next day we toured the city with the international group of enthusiastic travelers on our tour. But we couldn't keep our minds off the Bibles hidden in the closet of our hotel room. How were we going to get rid of them? Had anyone ever tried to carry them back across the border into Hong Kong? No, I felt God had assured me. Finally, we settled on the idea of attending a church in Canton and giving the Bibles away there.

That Sunday we were supposed to go with our tour group to the Pingchow People's Commune. However, I told the tour guide, "We want to go to church."

She said, "There are no churches in Canton."

"We have heard of a church here led by the Three Self Patriotic Movement," I replied. "We have the address here." I showed her a small piece of paper with an address scribbled on it. Since it was a government-approved church she allowed us to go. As far as we knew it was the only Christian church in the city. The Three Self church existed to show outsiders that China allowed religious freedom.

We packed sixty New Testaments in a carry-on bag, hailed a taxi, and arrived at the address we had been given. As we drove up, we could see the church's big iron gates were locked! Hesitantly, we got out of the car. We stood there for a few minutes wondering what to do next. A busy marketplace was nearby and streams of people dressed in navy blue Mao attire stared at us as they walked by carrying fresh fish and other strange looking items. Many seemed as if they had never seen a white foreigner. We felt vulnerable but not without faith. Finally, a little old Chinese woman with a big smile opened the gate to let us in. We had arrived well before the Sunday service time.

Desperate to be successful in our mission, we introduced ourselves to the pastors and announced, "We have Bibles." One replied, "Oh, we don't need Bibles. We print them here in China."

"Please take them anyway. It's our gift to your congregation." They reluctantly took them, then headed off to prepare for the service.

Soon we were sitting in the large church sanctuary, the only two white faces in a crowd of about 500 Chinese worshipers. During the service, Joyce and I decided we'd tell the pastors about the rest of the Bibles at the hotel. Probably not too smart considering the pastors' attitude, but we didn't know what else to do. After the service, we pushed through the crowd, looking for one of the church leaders.

Suddenly a loud, gregarious Chinese man dressed in Western clothes appeared out of the crowd in front of us. "Hello, I'm Dan Li from England."

"Oh, hi! We're Errol and Joyce Martens from Canada," I replied, relieved to be speaking English.

"I'm from a family of Christian Chinese immigrants," Dan said. "I'm here on business and decided to see what church is like in China. What brings you here?"

"We hear the believers here are desperate for Bibles," I said.

Suddenly, I felt a prompt to tell him we had Bibles and to invite him to our hotel room.

He didn't hesitate. "Thank you. I'd love to come."

Once in the taxi, I started to feel nervous about what I'd just done. *Who is this guy? Could he be a government agent?*

No sooner did we get into our hotel room with Dan when there was a knock at the door. I thought, *Oh no, it's the authorities. They've come to arrest us!* As I cautiously opened the door, there stood two young Chinese men. Our contacts! They said in broken English, "We so sorry. We went to wrong hotel the other night."

With Dan translating for us, we asked what life was like for Chinese Christians. "It's very hard," said one young man who identified himself as part of the underground church. "During the Cultural Revolution there was much persecution."

"Is there a need for more Bibles?"

"Oh yes, in my area, more than 300 people will share one Bible."

We opened the closet and dragged out our two huge bags. What joy we felt as we transferred the Bibles from our two full suitcases, into their empty ones. We felt it was such a small sacrifice on our part to be an answer to the prayers of the suffering church in China in this way. Joining hands, we prayed, and they left with Dan.

Two weeks later, we met Dan at the YMCA in Hong Kong. He was bursting with excitement. "Those Bibles made it to five destinations in China. Your delivery project was a victory." We rejoiced together and talked about China late into the evening.

After our China experience, we returned to our beloved little church in Langdon, Alberta, for a year and a half, and then returned to Asia with the YWAM Far East Evangelism Teams. But we didn't go alone. Our family had grown to three, and this time we brought our precious first-born daughter, Tanya.

As for ministry, we launched out with evangelism teams, Joyce served her cooking skills and I was invited to head up one of the ministries—Bibles to China. Over the next six months I oriented many visiting YWAM teams in this task. About 20 percent of our teams were stopped at the border, however, these couriers could pick up the confiscated Bibles on their way back out. All in all, over 10,000 of our Bibles made it to their destinations.

When facing overwhelming odds and accusing voices, King David had learned to declare God's name, trust in Him, and say with confidence, "But you, LORD, are a shield around me, my glory, the One who lifts my head high. From the LORD comes deliverance." (Psalm 3:3,8 NIV)

As it turned out, our experience with guidance, provision and deliverance in our 'China story' would be just the 'tip of the iceberg' in regards to the decades of missionary life that still lay before us.

Chapter 6

On to Greenland

After Asia, we settled in Edmonton, Alberta Canada with our little Tanya, and it was where her three precious siblings, Jayna, Angela, and Anthony would be born. But it was not where they would live some of their most formative years.

On the morning of November 26, 1982, just four months after arriving in Edmonton, I was alone in the YWAM office having personal quiet time. It was my habit to ask God each morning, "What country should I pray for today?" Then I'd pray for whatever country came to mind.

Instantly, I heard the word "Greenland." I sat there stiff as a statue for a few moments. I couldn't recall ever thinking about Greenland.

I got up off my chair to study the large world map hanging on the office wall. Greenland was a huge ice-covered island just off the northeast coast of Canada. *Are there even people there?* I wondered, *Of course, there must be. God wouldn't ask me to pray for rocks and snow!*

I prayed for Greenland that morning as I might have for any other country. But now I was curious and I started reading anything I could find about it.

A few months later, in a staff meeting, our leaders asked what was on our hearts for the coming season. When it came around to me, I said, "Greenland."

My answer was so far off everyone's grid that they couldn't help but burst out laughing. That confirmed I wasn't the only one who'd never thought of Greenland before. But our leader took it seriously. Shortly afterward, he approached Loren Cunningham at a conference in Washington. "There is a guy on our base who has a vision for Greenland...," he explained.

"Encourage him in it," Loren answered.

And he did. In 1984, I set out on a scouting trip to Greenland. At first, I had presumed someone would join me but soon realized this would be a solo journey. As I prayed and prepared, I felt I was not to take a sleeping bag. In Luke Chapter 10, when Jesus sent out his disciples, he told them what to take and what not to take. I felt that not taking a sleeping bag would symbolize my trust in God to take care of me. I didn't have a single contact in Greenland, so I truly needed his help. I did not have a credit card or a cell phone, and I had only enough money for three nights in a hotel, and the trip was scheduled to last three weeks!

The only passage I could find from Canada to Greenland was a once-a-week First Air flight from Iqaluit (far north of Montreal in the Nunavut territory of Canada). My flights took me from Edmonton to Montreal to Iqaluit and finally to Nuuk, the capital city of Greenland. The four-hour flight from Montreal to Iqaluit was my first visit to the Canadian Arctic. As I wandered around the isolated town of Iqaluit (now the capital of Nunavut), I came upon a building that was hard *not* to notice —the Anglican Church. It was built in the round shape and white color of a large igloo, the traditional snow house of the Canadian Inuit.

I stepped inside and was intrigued by the definitive Inuit style. The pulpit was made from an upturned dogsled, the prayer cushions were covered with seal skin, and on the walls were colorful pictures of Bible stories intertwined with scenes of Arctic life and culture. The vicar of the church greeted me warmly. After chatting a while, I asked a favor.

"I'm on my way over to Greenland," I said. My flight is leaving early in the morning. Would you mind if I caught a few hours' sleep inside the church?"

He welcomed me to do so, and that night I slept under some wooden benches, warm and already sensing God's provision. It felt like I had barely closed my eyes when my alarm jolted me awake at 2:15 a.m. in the morning

I stood up, rubbed my eyes, grabbed my bag and guitar, and began the 20-minute walk to the airport in the light of the midsummer Arctic sun. On that 4 a.m. flight I soon realized *why* there was only one plane a week to Greenland. There were just three passengers on our Twin Otter turboprop—a Japanese businessman, an elderly French artist, and me.

As the old plane lifted to its flying altitude and headed east of Iqaluit, the massive tundra came into view: bare rocks, patches of snow, and great pools of water from the yearly snow melt. As we reached the open water of the Davis Strait, the scene was even more breathtaking. The sun reflected off thousands of brilliant white ice floes contrasting against the dark sea in a seemingly infinite expanse.

"Wow, the landscape is so vivid in this clean, crisp Arctic air," I said as the two passengers and I piled into a taxi. Quaint, brightly painted houses dotted the rugged Nuuk peninsula. I saw patches of thick green grass on grey rocky outcrops and white-topped cotton-sedge in low-lying bogs. But there was not a single tree in sight! The rocky tundra cannot support tree growth and most of the year, snow covers the towns of Greenland, melting only during the long summer days—though the air is still chilly.

We arrived early in the day and after checking into my room at the Godthab Hotel, I set out into the town. Walking along, I prayed silently for people I passed on the streets. I also climbed the rocky hills nearby, reaching out my hands to pray over the city. I did many prayer walks and day by day, I felt my heart growing for the people of this isolated and unfamiliar land. At the same time, I was looking for someone I could connect with for mission purposes. The Bible calls this person "a man of peace" (Luke 10:6). But after two full days of looking for church buildings, praying, and knocking on doors, no "man of peace" appeared. Not only that, I had finances for only one more night in a hotel, and there were still nineteen days left on my scouting trip!

That night my mind wrestled with ideas of how to proceed. In my earlier research regarding Greenland missionaries, all I had found was one Pentecostal mission in Sisimiut. However, I had no contact information. A passenger ship was leaving for Sisimiut soon, but the fare was 1,200 Danish Kroner (about $150 US at the time)—which was almost all the money I had left. There was also no guarantee that there would be any space left on the vessel at this late date.

After enjoying a good supper I spent the whole evening praying. As I worshipped with my guitar, I felt excitement and peace about seeking out the Pentecostal missionary in Sisimiut.

The next morning I opened my Bible to the story of Jacob in Genesis. He too faced fearful possibilities (much worse than mine) as he returned from a far land. He had to meet his brother Esau, who years before had vowed to kill him. One night Jacob wrestled with God, but finally had a breakthrough. He had peace that he and his family would be okay. And they were.

It was now my third day in Greenland. My circumstances seemed grim, but there was a sense of joyful expectation in my spirit. I got ready to go into town with fresh confidence, even dressing with a tie!

On my walk, I noticed a blue building with a cross on it. I had knocked on the front door the previous day with no answer. I tried again today, and I was about to give up when I caught a glimpse of a person walking by the window. This time I went around to the back door.

When that door opened, it was like I had discovered the secret passage to a cavern of riches. The people inside were short-term missionaries from Denmark, assisting while the regular Mission House leaders were on vacation. Over tea and cookies, they told me about missions in Greenland and the spiritual needs of the people. During our conversation I couldn't help but ask, "Would you happen to have a phone number for that Pentecostal mission up in Sisimiut?" They did and offered me the telephone to use.

"Hello, my name is—" After identifying myself and my purpose, I waited for the reply. "Yes, yes, of course you can visit," came the cheerful

Swedish accent from the other end. "We don't get many visitors up here, especially from Canada. Come, come."

"By the way, what is your name?" I asked.

"Gunvor Åsblom."

"Thank you so much, Gunvor. I am looking forward to meeting you. There is a ship leaving Monday."

The good news didn't end there.

"Errol, would you like to join us for supper?" one of the Denmark missionaries asked. "And you can take the room upstairs until you leave for Sisimiut if you like."

"That will be wonderful!"

My steps were light and joyful as I walked back to the hotel to get my things. "Hallelujah! Thank you, Lord!" After returning to the Mission House, I walked upstairs and into a bright little room that was even more comfortable than the one I had at the Godthab Hotel. I spent the rest of the afternoon praying and dreaming about a future outreach in Greenland.

When I bought my ticket for the ship to Sisimiut, the ticket agent handed it to me with a warning: "There is no guarantee you'll get on board with this economy ticket because it is all sold out. I also need to tell you the ship is waylaid because of ice floes and won't leave until late tonight."

My new friends accompanied me to the harbor that evening, and as I walked up the gangplank of the *Kununnguaq*, I could see them waving goodbye. I was on! Again, the words of Psalm 3 came to mind, "from the Lord comes deliverance."

The INO Church Mission House in Nuuk, 1984

CHAPTER 7

Our First Arctic Outreach

THE WEATHER HAD been grey that first week in Greenland. But close to midnight, while standing on the ship's open deck, the polar sun burst through the broken clouds. Dazzling orange exploded across the sky and water illuminating everything in sight including a majestic iceberg which shone like a sapphire in the distance. I was awestruck.

Around noon the next day, the passenger liner deftly navigated into the Sisimiut harbor. The sky was brilliant blue, and the sunshine glistened on the town's colorful, steep-roofed wooden houses perched on the rocky terrain.

Two friendly talkative Dutch women greeted me at the wharf. A small taxi chauffeured us up a steep winding road. Within three minutes, we'd stopped in front of a large yellow building with a sign above its white door that said, ZIONSBORG, (House of Zion).

Once inside, one of the women said to me, "God put Greenland on our hearts about a year and a half ago. We were praying about which people group to pursue. We had never thought of Greenland before."

"Wow, that's much like what happened to me," I said. "Also about a year and a half ago!"

The women showed me to a small room adjacent to the church sanctuary that we later came to call 'the prophet's chamber.' The window looked over a green valley swooping down toward the fjord. Jagged gray mountains towered over the other side. Echoing off the rocks, I heard the howling and whining of sled dogs chained in their teams throughout the valley.

For my first supper, the women served seal meat. This staple in the Greenlandic diet has the texture of beef but is black in color and has a fishy liver taste.

"The meat is lean, high in protein, and very rich in B Vitamins," they added. The next day, we ate dried fish and raw seal fat on our visit with an elderly Greenlandic woman. I first balked at the seal fat but was surprised at how melt-in-your-mouth tasty it was. Nothing at all like beef fat.

The highly respected Greenland author Robert Petersen once wrote, "It is the common understanding that to have a Greenlandic identity a person must eat dried meat, dried fish, raw mattak, etc. Not only should the person be able to eat it, he or she should also like it (which is not so difficult)." Raw mattak is greatly relished as a traditional food. Mattak is the dark outer skin of either a bowhead or beluga whale which is sliced together with an inch (2.5 cm) or so of light colored blubber. The fat is typically cut into small cubes still attached to the skin and these small chunks are chewed to extract the flavor and nutrients. It soon becomes like a bit of chewing gum which is either swallowed or discarded when the taste is gone.

Thankfully, I enjoyed the wild meats of Greenland. Who could not like a reindeer roast, musk ox steak, or fish soup? It is delicious. However, there were some Greenlandic delicacies a foreigner might resist—like raw, bloody seal liver. I did eat it, but I admit, I enjoyed the smiles of approval from my Greenlandic hosts more than the taste!

I soon met Gunvor, the cheerful Swedish woman I'd spoken to on the phone. "Errol, so nice you could come. Welcome. Can you come up to join my husband, Rune, and me for coffee around eight o'clock this evening?"

"Yes. I look forward to it."

Gunvor seemed amazed that YWAM sent out young people as missionaries. "I want you to meet a Lutheran priest in south Greenland who has been favorable to our evangelistic work. He's born-again, and I think he might be someone your YWAM teams could work with."

"He sounds like quite a remarkable person. From what I've heard, the priests in Greenland often speak openly against other Christian workers who are not under the State Church."

"That's true, but this man is different."

"What is his name?" I asked.

"It's Palasi (Pastor) Sven Russell."

As she said the name, my ears perked up. I remembered an intercessory prayer time with the Discipleship Training School small group shortly before I left on this trip. I'd asked the group, "Would you pray with me and ask the Lord for any words He might have for me before I go?"

We bowed our heads, quietened our hearts, and listened. After a few moments of silence, each one shared their impressions. When I came around to one 18-year-old student, he said, "I got the name, Sven."

Hmmm. Was this Lutheran priest going to be a key person in our future work in Greenland?

Later, in our conversation Gunvor said, "Perhaps your team could go along with our oldest son from village to village in his new boat next summer. He usually goes in July."

"That sounds great!" I said. "What's his name?" "His name is Sven too, Sven-Olov. He would be the one to be in touch with about coming next summer."

I thought to myself, *That is a name I won't forget!*

"Gunvor, I definitely will be in touch with your son."

The doors for ministry in Sisimiut were open, but a new obstacle emerged. Unexpectedly, my ship back to Nuuk had to dock for repairs. When I learned the next ship was fully booked, I became concerned I would miss that once-a-week flight back to Canada. After a tense couple of days, a seat opened up on a helicopter. I didn't have enough money for the fare, but I reserved it with faith. Miraculously, as I was walking down the road with Gunvor and Rune's youngest son, David, he unexpectedly handed me sufficient money to pay for the trip!

That evening, I had supper in Nuuk with Dan and Gudrun Toldam, the Danish missionaries who were the official overseers of the blue Mission House where I had stayed two weeks earlier. Over a succulent meal of *Frikadeller* (Danish meatballs), potatoes, and red cabbage, I shared my vision.

"Since I've been here, my heart has been stirred by the potential impact an outreach team could have. I want to bring one. What do you think?"

"That sounds like a good idea," said Dan. "Perhaps some of our Greenlandic youth could join you and learn some of your evangelistic dramas?"

"Oh, for sure."

"It should be possible to visit some of the schools in town," said Gudrun. "Classes resume mid-August. And, we know it is expensive to travel to Greenland from Canada so if you come with a team, we'd be happy to pay for your meals."

Dan and Gudrun's encouragement sent my heart soaring with joy and gratitude. Yet as I returned to the guest room I wondered, "Had I done enough on this trip? Had I missed anything important?"

Even in my times of doubt and insecurity, I felt God's presence, encouragement, guidance, and provision. And as it turned out, there were only two nights out of the three week trip I could have used a sleeping bag, and that was not a hardship!

* * *

The ten months leading up to the first Greenland outreach were a flurry of activity. Besides putting together the outreach I still had other responsibilities at YWAM Edmonton. I also wanted to spend as much time as possible with Joyce and our children.

We now had a team of fifteen eager participants for that Greenland team. There were thirteen Canadians, one American, and one Hollander—eleven women and four men. Their ages spanned 18 to 33. We divided into a South Team, which I led, and a North Team, led by two YWAMers and the *Evangelisten* boat captain, Sven-Olov Åsblom. He was the Sven God was leading us to throughout that prayer time in Edmonton. What a blessing he turned out to be!

We began the outreach with nine training days at the YWAM base in Turner Valley, Alberta. We spent those days in intercessory prayer for Greenland, drama practice, testimony preparation, and inspirational Bible teaching. It took three days for our teams to travel to Greenland. When our South Team landed at Nuuk airport, our weary hearts leapt at the sight of the awe-inspiring coastline and snow-capped mountains.

I noticed a different flag flying over homes and businesses as we drove from the airport. I asked our driver about it. He said, “It’s our new Greenlandic flag, commemorating the 1979 establishment of home rule and greater sovereignty from Denmark.”

We started with great excitement, but one day early on I noticed a team member exhibiting signs of depression. I asked the team, “Is anyone feeling down?” Sure enough, about half the team said yes. Through openness, prayer, and worship, that heaviness soon lifted and the team was filled with faith.

Our first outreach venue was a summer youth camp far up the fjord. We arrived at the camp dock after a four-hour boat ride, just in time to minister in the evening meeting. Inside the lodge we had a captive audience of twenty-five preteen boys.

After the meeting our team started chatting in the dining room. Someone said, “Why don’t we hold Bible clubs in Nuuk as a follow-up for the kids going through this camp?” It seemed like a great idea. So after returning to Nuuk, we organized a four-day club which attracted many children and youth.

Our next big adventure was a 40-hour voyage along the craggy coastline to Narsaq, a town 250 nautical miles south of Nuuk. Because of the turbulent Arctic waters, many of the team were seasick but everyone bounced back once we docked and started preparing for a scheduled children’s meeting. When the set time arrived, the local missionary opened the chapel doors and a crowd of kids and teens flooded in. He said, “Wow, this is the biggest crowd I’ve seen since I arrived in Greenland two years ago.”

No one on our team could speak Greenlandic or even Danish, and few of the Greenlandic kids could speak English. Thank God he sent us Lis Hansen, a 20-year-old Greenlander with a quick smile and a heart for Jesus. She did a great job translating for us. One day I said to her,

"Lis, someday we'll run a Discipleship Training School in Greenland. I'd like you to join." She was eager.

We spread seeds of the gospel in different settings, and some souls in Narsaq were already ripe for harvest. One of those was a Greenlandic man in his early twenties. He said to me, "I have received new life. Light has come into my life. I am so thankful!"

In the meantime, the North Team had their own adventures in ministry and on the high seas. The *Evangelisten* broke down north of Nuuk, in Maniitsoq and the team ended up staying there for three weeks. They spent those weeks ministering in open-air meetings and at the Maniitsoq Mission House.

Sven finally decided to move the team to Sisimiut using a smaller speed boat. He'd done the six-hour trip many times, but he was still concerned about the rough seas at the mouth of the huge Kangerlussuaq Fjord. As they set off, the water was calm. But after the boat left the protection of rocky islands near the coastline, wind strength increased and the waves grew. Freezing salt spray doused the shivering team. Sven shouted over the roar of the motor and waves, "Hey, pull this tent over yourselves."

One team member told us later, "We thought we would die out there. Then we were worried we *wouldn't* die, and our terror would go on forever."

Finally, Sven noticed a small rocky island with an abandoned cabin. He let the team off and said, "Hold tight, I'll be back tomorrow." As they watched him speed away through the terrifying waves they prayed, "Oh Lord, keep him safe. No one else knows we are here!" Sven had spent most of his life sailing on restless waves so it was a thrill ride for him. But on that day, the thrill was eclipsed by concern for his foreign guests.

When our two teams reconnected later that month in the Nuuk Mission House, we all talked and laughed about our incredible adventures. The hottest topic was the North Team's ride of terror. Yes, Sven kept his word and returned to pick up the team the next day. One of the young Canadian girls declared, "I kissed the ground as soon as we arrived in Sisimiut!"

Others exclaimed, "Did you guys get to eat any seal meat and seagull soup—We did!" The North team was in awe of its fearless Captain

Sven—his skill with a boat, knowledge of the Greenlandic language, and endless pranks. Our two teams had shared the gospel with hundreds of students in Greenland schools, just as Dan and Gudrun had predicted. The national television station got wind of our presence and wanted to do a fifteen-minute presentation on television. We filmed it at the Nuuk airport, right on the tarmac. Our teams performed three of our action songs and two short dramas for the camera crew. The next day a reporter came to interview Dan Toldam and me.

Our team had come to Greenland to share our testimonies wherever we found an opportunity. In this case, the opportunity came to us, and it was national TV! This first outreach to Greenland was a great lesson for me in how much God loves missions. We were an inexperienced group of youth stepping into unknown territory, and God was with us. He opened doors for us, supplied all our needs, and touched many hearts through our simple efforts of faith.

The outreach wasn't entirely a happy memory. A few times, we were jeered, cursed, and spattered with eggs. One night our girls, who were all sleeping on the floor in the Mission House, were startled awake by loud banging on the piano. It turned out to be a drunken man who was the only Greenlandic member of the Nuuk, Mission House then.

Depression and alcoholism had reached epidemic proportions in Greenland. Many believed these and other social ills were triggered by rapid modernization, which had upset Greenland's well-established cultural norms. While we were in Nuuk, more and more youth came to hang around us, and a number received Christ. However, we didn't realize how broken and hurting most of these youth were.

At the end of the outreach, it touched us deeply to hear Dan Toldam say, "Please come back next year. It has been very, very good to have you here. New doors have opened for our ministry."

I was overwhelmed. "Dan, what could we have done without you and Gudrun! Thank you so much for your encouragement and generosity."

We would *definitely* bring more teams, but a new vision was brewing that would take us even farther.

Our outreach team on the Nuuk airport runway performing for the national T.V. production

Chapter 8

The Big Launch

THE FOLLOWING SUMMER I was back in Greenland planning a future outreach. I had just arrived in Narsaq, South Greenland when I got an unexpected call from YWAM's International Office in Kona, Hawaii.

"Hello Errol, I am Loren Cunningham's assistant. I'm calling to let you know that Loren and his wife Darlene will be visiting Nuuk from August 14 to 16. Will you be there?"

"Yes. I'm in Greenland now. A YWAM outreach team will be arriving in Nuuk soon, too. We'll all look forward to the Cunningham's visit!"

Loren and Darlene Cunningham are the founders of Youth With A Mission, and I was eager to talk with them about our pioneering work in Greenland and about starting a DTS there. Within a few hours of arriving in Nuuk, after the 2 day ship journey from Narsaq, I received another unexpected phone call. It was Joyce. She'd been bravely holding down the fort at home but ran into some overwhelming concerns.

"Errol, I'm feeling lots of pressure here. The car broke down, we have bills to pay, and I don't know what to do with all the staff. We have no office for them. I also need to get Tanya registered for first grade. I wish you were here."

Joyce's momentary desperation left me upset and worried because I wouldn't be home for three more weeks. I found some quiet time with the Lord and didn't leave until I came to a place of peace. In those next three weeks, God provided all the resources and help that Joyce needed. When Joyce called again, she had even bigger news.

"Errol, I just got back from the medical clinic. We are having another baby!"

"Wow," I replied after a moment of stunned silence, "That's wonderful!"

After discussing the new baby's expected arrival, I said, "Loren will be with us here in Nuuk in a few days, and I intend to talk to him about starting a DTS. What do you think?"

Joyce hesitated, "Well, with our third baby coming in March, I'm not sure how our family can be involved, but our lives certainly haven't been ordinary so far."

* * *

On August 14 I woke up feeling weary. I'd been away from my family for thirty-seven days with a week still to go! I was feeling stressed as I anticipated the summer team's return to Nuuk, the Cunningham visit, and all the needs at home.

Later that day, I received another unexpected call at the mission house. A friendly voice said, "Hi Errol, it's Loren Cunningham. My flight has been delayed until Sunday. Because of this change Darlene can't be with me. If you don't think it is good timing, I could just fly over Greenland and be on my way."

"Oh no," I replied. "We want you to come. I'll be here along with a small YWAM outreach team. The Mission House leaders are looking forward to meeting you. They have a place for you to stay."

That same evening, Sven and the Summer of Service team arrived on the *Evangelisten* from the Northern villages. One team member presented me with a 31-page report on their adventures. I was delighted to hear that Ha Nguyen, who had been leading the YWAM refugee ministry in Edmonton and living with our family, had such a successful outreach. Ha had been a refugee himself and had an incredible testimony of his escape from communism in Vietnam.

Ha and the team had a good chuckle out of an English gaffe he made while sharing his testimony in one village.

Ha quoted Luke 6:29 where Jesus said, "If someone takes your coat, do not withhold your shirt from them." But he made a small error and said, "If someone takes your coat, give him also your *underwear*."

Knowing Ha's generous nature, I wouldn't be surprised at him giving away his last item.

Loren arrived Sunday evening as scheduled, and within a couple of hours, he was up preaching in the Mission House. The next day he joined our small team for some open-air evangelism. It was cloudy, a chilly wind was blowing, and some in the crowd were drunk. We had no visible response to our preaching, but I knew some hearts had been touched.

Later, Loren said to me, "Since I've been here in Nuuk, I've heard several times that 'Greenland is a hard mission field!' Don't say, 'It is a hard mission field.' Rather, say, 'We just haven't found the key yet.' If God intended to reach Greenland in the way we thought, it would be evangelized already! But rather ask the Lord for his ideas for reaching Greenland."

One afternoon, Loren joined Sven and me in the *Evangelisten's* small dining table. The ocean was gently rocking us as Loren asked Sven questions about Greenland. Then he turned to me. "Errol, you said you had something on your mind you wanted to discuss."

"Yes, I have been praying about starting a DTS here. Sven and I have discussed it, and I want to run it by you. I've helped lead these schools in Edmonton but starting one in a foreign country seems like such a big task with a lot of unknowns."

Loren turned to Sven. "How big is the Mission House? About how many people could it hold for running a school?"

"It's a refurbished army barrack with sleeping room for about twenty to thirty people."

After Sven's answer, Loren said, "You'll be looking at about fourteen students. Aim to have half of them Greenlanders and half foreigners. The students will learn from each other and develop heart connections with other nations."

"As for teachers, have the bigger, well-established YWAM bases support this pioneering work by sending a teacher and paying their travel. The Greenland base should cover their room and board. Our base in Hawaii could send Paul Hawkins. He's one of our best. Your teachers should be dynamic, imparting annointing to the students, not just content. Minister identity to the Greenlanders. Bring in participants from other Indigenous people groups, both teachers and students."

I was stunned. What I saw as a distant possibility, Loren was bringing to reality. We prayed together about when we might start the school. While listening quietly for God's impressions, Loren received the verse 2 Samuel 11:1, "In the spring, at the time when kings go off to war..." So Loren affirmed a spring start. Sven was willing but I was still needing more confirmation. Joyce was due to give birth mid March.

God soon made it clear he *did* want me to launch the DTS in Greenland. Though we were expecting our third child, Joyce was committed to moving our whole family there. We began to plan and raise funds for the school. Already in the area, Rune Åsblom was able to be our special speaker at the "Gospel-to-Greenland" fundraising breakfast. Speaking in Swedish through an interpreter, Rune wowed the crowd with his missionary stories. After that I shared my vision. Donations poured in. When all was counted we found ourselves amply supplied.

Rune flew back to Greenland with us. In all, sixteen of us left Canada together for the DTS, including our daughters Tanya (age 7), Jayna (age 4), and newborn Angela. On March 31 we boarded the ship in Nuuk and headed for the Arctic Circle. Our destination was Sisimiut, the northernmost town considered ice-free for winter travel. Ice-free, however, did not mean there was no ice. It just meant the ship could usually cut through it.

While the rest of the team slept in the open bunk rooms on the top deck, Joyce settled comfortably in a berth in the hull of the *Kununguaq* with two-week-old Angela cradled in her arms. After midnight she was startled awake by the roar of powerful diesel engines throttling forward.

The ship shuddered as giant pieces of ice grated against the hull next to her cabin. All night, the icebreaker hammered its bow into the ice. The engines' constant vibration and noise made Joyce terrified she would end up in the frozen sea with her newborn, just like the heroine of the Eugenia Price novel she was reading.When we arrived, my heart was soaring. My family had now entered the Greenland experience with me. The sky was brilliant blue as it had been the first summer I'd come. However, this time the town was sparkling white. Sled dogs were howling, and their mushers were driving them, kicking up great clouds of snow. Children squealed in delight as they sleighed down the hill. Soon Tanya and Jayna were joining in the fun.

The first-ever YWAM Discipleship Training School class in Greenland was now sitting before me in the Zionsburg Mission House—five Greenlanders and six foreigners, including one Swede, one Norwegian, and four Canadians. I was especially pleased that Lis Hansen, our interpreter from the first outreach, was enrolled.

Our Swedish student hadn't planned on taking the DTS. He had come to visit and help around Zionsborg. While hiking in the mountains, he fell and broke his foot. Since he couldn't work, he started attending the lectures where God touched his heart. In the DTS, he also met his future wife, Greenlandic Lis!

Dave and Liz Skene from Ontario helped us co-lead the school, and we found ourselves with plenty of decisions to make. Fortunately, Dave and I had a similar mindset as we both loved to pray and often received the same answers from the Lord. Later, we would include the students when praying for direction.

Scott Smith, who had been one of the guys on our '85 outreach team, volunteered to join our staff for this first DTS as our full-time cook and leadership support. Scott had an incredible testimony of how he got his five-year call to Greenland.

"I came upon an article by Errol Martens, who had just completed his first trailblazing trip to Greenland. As I read the article, the Holy Spirit gripped my heart about what God wanted to do there. I was barely halfway into the article when I felt this supernatural joy about being involved … The amazing part was that I was brain-damaged as a baby and had only one emotion—a sort of 'middle of the road' contentment.

I did not know sadness or laughter or great joy. This new vision and call sparked a strong emotion that I felt for the first time. I knew God was speaking and had gripped my heart with a vision."

Our first teacher, Teo van der Weele from Holland, wowed the students with stories of faith, courage, and forgiveness from his days living under Nazi rule in Holland during World War ll. Our second teacher was Paul Martinson from Vancouver. Paul had written to me, "Our YWAM group spent the morning praying for Greenland, you, and the upcoming DTS. We also upheld Joyce and the new addition to your family. Perhaps the Lord will send along a nanny to minister to your family while in Greenland." Paul's words proved prophetic as God did send a nanny. In his letter, Paul offered to teach in our school. He was a godsend. He would become a regular teacher in our DTS and encourager of the ministry to this day.

And true to his word, Loren sent Paul Hawkins from Kona as the third outside teacher. He, too, challenged the students to go deeper than ever before in trusting God. He modeled the discipline of seeking and listening to God's voice and practicing generosity.

We recorded all the lectures. Loren urged me the year before, "Buy a video camera and record all the lectures in both languages." These video lectures would become so valuable in future schools. It seemed impossible to fill each week of the three-month lecture phase of the school with live teachers in such a remote location. But with some on-site teachers, some video lectures, and some teaching weeks by our staff, it all worked out.

Besides the lectures, each visiting teacher spent significant time with the staff and students at meals and in one-on-one conversations. We would need all the spiritual insight we could get for the next phase of the school—the outreach. As Sven took us south from Sisimiut on the *Evangelisten*, we unknowingly headed straight into danger. A great obstacle loomed ahead, and another great opportunity to experience God's deliverance.

Loren and Sven-Olov on the Evangelisten in the Nuuk harbour.

Chapter 9

All the Way South

LAUNCHING THE OUTREACH had taken weeks of preparation. Everyone practiced the dramas, songs, and testimonies we'd be presenting for ministry along the coast. Students also helped with sanding, painting, and fixing up the mission boat in dry dock. Most importantly, we all prepared in prayer.

On June 28, the full-to-capacity *Evangelisten* cast off from the Nuuk harbor. After we'd gone a few miles out to sea, Sven called the school to attention. First in Greenlandic and then in English, he gave a few simple rules for life and safety on board. Even in summer, it was cold at sea, and we soon took refuge inside the boat's small dining room.

Sven piloted the boat all night. During a short stop in Paamiut, I called Joyce and then our missionary contacts in Narsaq, where we were headed.

We continued south through abundant ice floes. Late that evening, Sven anchored behind some rocky islands where the water was calm as glass. We stopped our activities for the day and went to bed, but those ice floes didn't stop. They silently moved into position like a conquering army surrounding our boat, and herein I return to my stuck-in-the-ice story.

As we awoke and gathered on deck, a group of us decided to climb the mountain near the shoreline to get a better take on our situation. When we got high enough for a good view, we all went silent. We could see no open water at all. We were trapped.

Back on board all sixteen of us assembled. We were nine men and seven women from four nationalities, including six Greenlanders.

"Hey everyone," I said through interpretation, "From the mountain up there, we could only see solid white in every direction. It looks like we are completely trapped, but do you recall how the Lord spoke so clearly to us, with confirmation from Paul Hawkins?"

"Kujataamut" (to south), our most outspoken student replied.

"Now, Sven is the authority over this boat and over us related to safety. The final decision is his. But after discussing it with him, he is willing to keep pushing south. Are we in full agreement?" Everyone nodded yes, and we prepared for takeoff.

Some began worshipping the Lord with the guitar, another tried to help move ice with a pike pole, and one of our students, who'd had some experience on boats in Greenland, climbed the mast to get a better view. He shouted instructions to Sven when he saw better possibilities for maneuvering. But we moved only a short distance over the next two hours. Just before lunch, Sven decided to anchor. We stayed put over eight hours, praying, talking, and surveying our eerie and intimidating wilderness surroundings. We also rehearsed outreach strategies, as there was a positive expectancy on board, balanced with caution. "Go easy on the water supply," Sven warned before launching again.

After another hour of slow going, we broke into a narrow open channel in the ice. Cheers and laughter went up as Sven announced he was putting the throttle "full fart south." In Danish, "fart" means "speed" and "fart-plan" means "time-table." Visitors often laughed when we studied a passenger ship's "Fart-Plan."

Sven again sailed all night. About 5 a.m. I awakened to a startling CLUNK-GRIND-CLUNK-GRIND sound as the bow plowed through heavy chunks of ice. "That can't be good for this wooden boat," I whispered to myself.

Resolutely, we accelerated forward, tediously advancing, hour after hour. We heaved a collective "ahhh" sound whenever we hit open water. And more groans when the boat encountered another battalion of ice-soldiers!

Much of this kind of ice originates in the winter months in the northeast. Because frozen water is denser than liquid water, ice always floats. The warmer spring weather breaks the ice into massive chunks, which winds and ocean currents push south. The currents then move the ice around the south tip of Greenland and north, partway up the west coast. We experienced this natural phenomenon head-on. It felt like we were moving two steps forward and one back, but we were making headway. At midday, a solid white sheet of ice loomed before us as far as we could see. My heart sank. We couldn't help wondering. "Lord, how will this turn out?"

The *Evangelisten* seemed so tiny and powerless compared to the awesome force of nature around us. And yet, we were trusting in the all-powerful God who created it. Suddenly, we heard a noise in the sky above us. It was an airplane, and the pilot's voice on our radio gave us an explosion of hope.

"I can see open water toward the coastline," a voice crackled through the boat's small speaker, "Sail in an easterly direction toward land. You will hit the open water and be able to follow it out of the ice."

What a gift his words were to us! In the Bible, the word hope means "a confident expectation of good things."

When we broke through, calm, open waters and towering majestic icebergs welcomed us. What a relief to see Sven crank the engine to full fart! At one o'clock the next morning, we pulled up to the dock in Narsaq. It was an adventure none of us could forget and a powerful lesson in hearing God, acting in faith, persevering, and watching the Lord provide a friendly guiding voice in the sky. Because it was so late, we slept on the boat. We would see our hosts in the morning. We had made it all the way "South." And all the way out of the ice.

Most snow in south Greenland had melted by the time we arrived, and flocks of sheep and goats were grazing on the green hills around

Narsaq. The only farms in Greenland are here in the far south. The great Viking explorer, Eric the Red, settled in this area with Norsemen from Iceland around 1000 A.D. and by 1100 AD there were 300 farms in the region. Sadly, by late 1400 A.D. they had disappeared, likely because of a cooling period making farming too difficult

Narsaq is sheltered among a maze of fjords, inlets, and rocky islands, with remote villages dotting the long and lonely fjords. We tried to get to as many of these villages as we could during the eighteen days we were in the area. One of the most memorable for us was the picturesque village of Eqalugaarsuit. We began with a children's meeting that included puppets, songs, and a gospel message. Next, we challenged the villagers to a football (soccer) match. Then in the evening, we had a gospel meeting.

The outreach that day was a great success. The children's meeting produced many happy faces of both children and adults. The football match was like a wild rodeo, with twenty-four of us running back and forth, laughing, dust flying, spectators cheering. Even though our DTS had some fine players, the town won 5-3. At 7 p.m. about fifty people from the village crammed into its meeting hall for our dramas, testimonies, singing, and a short gospel message.

Unlike other places, where the people scattered after the meeting ended, most of the folks in Eqalugaarsuit hung around to sing, talk, and pray. We'd brought joy and hope to the villagers that day. While sailing back to Narsaq, we spotted an enormous iceberg. I said to Sven, "Hey, can you let Dave and I off here in the little boat? I want to take a picture of the *Evangelisten* in front of that magnificent iceberg."

Sven said, "Sure," but I should have noticed the prankster glint in his eye. After I took my picture, he revved the boat's engine and came full fart directly toward us. I watched the boat coming closer, horrified that it wasn't slowing down. I lifted an oar from our little skiff and jammed it against the hull of the *Evangelisten*, hoping to avoid impact. It was too close and too big! Instinctively, I dropped into the freezing water fully clothed! Watching from the deck above, Tanya burst into tears, and Sven turned pale. A collective gasp went up from the DTS team. "Errol's in the water," someone shouted. Meanwhile, Dave sat calmly in the boat, holding the video camera while I was fully submerged.

Though my parka was soaked, I managed to pop back into the little boat. However, it was not quick enough to avoid the sea water's bone-chilling bite or save the camera in my parka's pocket. As shocking as it was, the whole incident would provide lots of friendly banter for years to come.

Good days like we had in Eqalugaarsuit were sometimes followed by a sense of oppression and disunity. Like on July 14. I wanted to abandon ship and get out of there, and I wasn't the only one.

Our team included two troubled teenagers who joined us after the DTS had begun. One was 18-year-old Johannes, whose parents had both died. Sven took him under his wing and invited him to live with us in Sisimiut. Johannes came forward to receive Christ at one of our meetings and later joined the school. He had a gift of humor and was a delight to have around, but the DTS schedule was a culture shock for him. He was forever sleeping in and late for meetings. He constantly felt the tug of his old 'free" life, while at the same time didn't want it. Several of our other students had similar struggles. Then there was 16-year-old Jacob from the Nuuk Boys Home. Sven invited him on the outreach as a deckhand, but his belligerent attitude was wearing on us. Then something wonderful happened.

Around midnight on the day I wanted to jump ship, Jacob came to me asking for prayer. By 3:30 a.m., he had poured out a life of pain, including a long scroll of sins and guilt. "Jacob, are you ready to leave it all with Jesus?" Rutt interpreted for me. "Yes, I am." I led him in a prayer for salvation, and the next day Jacob's countenance was different.

This pattern continued through the DTS—exhilarating experiences one minute and tense moments the next—like the day we had a near mutiny in Qaqortoq. "We don't like this town," some students said. "And we don't want to hand out any magazines here." I was caught offguard for a moment, not knowing what to say. After a quick, silent prayer, an idea came to mind. "Okay," I said, "You have three minutes to pray and decide if you should go out or not. If not, fine, you can stay here and rest on the boat." Surprisingly, they all went out and had a good time.

On July 16th our team celebrated Tanya's eighth birthday with cake, games and lots of fun. Tanya even got to ride an Icelandic pony.

Later in the day, however, the mood shifted for me in a leaders meeting between Dave and I where he confronted me. It was one of the few tense moments between us, but a 'pearl' came out of it!

"Errol," "I feel like you just brushed off something important. Like I said before, I think we should seize teaching moments with the students as opportunities arise."

I was stunned and humbled. "Yes, I guess I have bulldozed ahead—partly because I didn't want to be stuck on the boat for hours going over complaints. I thought just going out into the villages would be better for morale—and for reaching the lost."

"I'm not thinking of us sitting on the boat for hours like that," Dave replied, "I simply want you to take time when a teaching moment arises."

"You're right, Dave. I need to get better at making space for that."

A few minutes after our meeting, a student who had been holding back his burdens was now ready to talk. This was more of a counseling moment, but like Dave said, "These opportunities can't be scheduled—they need to be seized upon when they arise."

On July 17 the whole DTS gathered around the missionary couple who had hosted our outreach. After praying over and blessing them and a few others there, the young wife shared her feelings, "We are so glad you came. It was significant for the town to see Greenlanders following Jesus."

Egede who lived in Narsaq was also sitting in that circle as we prayed. He had been our first convert from the first outreach. Now, two years later, he had joined in the outreach with our DTS—boldly sharing what the Lord had done for him.

Before sailing to Nuuk, we ministered in three more villages. As in all the other villages, we had good turnouts, strong presentations, and riveted listeners, but not the visible responses we'd hoped for. Although we believed God had impacted lonely hearts, it was not easy for them to step out and be different, especially in a small village where everyone knew each other.

Nevertheless, we'd seen signs of new life—the changed lives of our Greenlandic DTS students and the heartfelt prayers of villagers who'd responded during the outreach. It was a season of plowing and sowing, but more nurturing would be required. The challenge here was reflected in the words of a 25-year-old woman two of our team members had met in a small village. "I am a believer now," she said, "but it is hard here, and I feel so alone."

We sailed all night back to Nuuk. High waves battered our boat, sweeping seawater over the deck and relentlessly clanging pots and pans in the galley. We didn't sleep much that night, but somehow Sven managed to guide us securely back to the harbor in Nuuk. As we stepped out of the crowded cabin of the boat, the fresh, cool fragrance of the salty ocean air greeted us, as well as our loved ones.

Back at the Mission House, Joyce said, "Errol, after you and Tanya left, Jayna was so lonely. She is attached to her big sister, and they had never been separated before this trip. I'm struggling too. It has been a huge culture shock to live so closely in these new surroundings and to take care of our new baby. These long times away will affect our family relationships. We need to spend more time with just our family."

I reached out to hold her. "Yes, I want that too."

Despite its challenges, everyone felt the DTS was a great success and a lifetime memory. We'd blazed a trail and modeled what could be done with these kinds of schools.

"DTS has made me understand what it is to be a Christian," one student said, "It has strengthened me a lot… passing on the Good News…knowing about intercessory prayer… I learned something good from every teacher. I always used to feel guilty, but now I have a new understanding."

Another said, "When I get home, I'll see if I've really changed."

Yes, that is the test of true transformation—will it last?

As the DTS neared its conclusion, our family headed back to Canada. Dave stayed on in leadership to wrap up the school. After arriving back in Edmonton, we enjoyed vacation time as a family, but soon the ministry preparation started again.

We now had completed four consecutive years of YWAM ministry in Greenland, and it was growing each year. The next season would see another DTS and more outreaches. With all the projects in Alberta and Greenland, I wasn't looking for more to do. But there was another unexpected adventure waiting for me, in another territory I'd never heard of, 1,000 miles (1600 km) north of the Arctic Circle.

Rest stop after battling the first battalion of "Ice-Soldiers"

CHAPTER 10

Journey to the Top of the World

BECAUSE I WAS now on the YWAM map, I would often receive requests for information concerning ministry opportunities in Greenland. These requests came from countries far and near. I received requests from two ministries well known for their effectiveness. I envisioned many ways they could bless Greenland, but although we discussed, prayed, and even planned, these outreaches did not materialize. One that did move forward proved to be a remarkable adventure of faith for me.

In July 1987, Loren Cunningham sent out *Leader Letter #15*. He said YWAM had so far trailblazed for Christ in all but two of the 223 countries of the world. The letter also mentioned that there were still a handful of territories YWAM had not yet reached with ministry teams. One of those was Svalbard, a group of islands northeast of Greenland with a Norwegian and Russian population.

Loren's letter encouraged us to pray about this challenge. "Please let me know immediately if you plan to go into one of these countries or territories," he wrote. British YWAMer Phil Gazley and I prayed and felt called to take on Svalbard. After much contemplation, we set our plans for July 1988.

We were eager to go, but the Svalbard trip had to wait. Over the next few months, I helped with interim leadership of the YWAM Turner Valley base in southern Alberta, worked on several projects for the upcoming DTS in Sisimiut, and helped train two East Greenland outreach teams at the YWAM base in Dunham, Quebec. From there, Phil and I would launch our much-anticipated trip to the top of the world.

Our two-day journey took us through Ottawa, Montreal, London, Oslo, and then to the world's northernmost civilian airport, Svalbard. We were now a thousand miles (1600 km) north of the Arctic Circle and just 650 miles (1040) from the North Pole.

Svalbard's rocky islands were shaped by mountains, glaciers, and fjords. At that time, the population was 3,600—about 1,200 were Norwegians and another 2,000 Soviet citizens. Norway had full sovereignty of the area, but forty countries had signed a treaty allowing them to mine the islands' coal and minerals.

Upon landing at the small, windswept Longyearbyen Airport, we asked a well-dressed Norwegian man, "Can you tell us where the campground is?"

"Yes, it's just down there, toward the fjord, not far from the airport," he answered with a smile.

The campground looked vacant, bleak, and rocky, but Phil was undaunted. "Hey Errol, this looks like a good spot." We set up our tent in a howling wind. "Brrr, it's chilly," I said with a shudder, "I'm getting on my winter coat and windbreaker pants."

"Me too," Phil replied. "Then let's hightail it into town."

It was a four-kilometer walk into Longyearbyen (the Norwegian town). We hoped to find gas for our camp stove, but none was available. We did get a hot meal at the town's restaurant and then returned to our tent. I had intentionally brought an extra warm sleeping bag for this trip, having learned my lesson from a scouting trip in East Greenland two years before where we'd camped for two weeks, and I'm sure glad I did! Our three objectives for Svalbard were to:

1. Do research in preparation for future ministry
2. Conduct a door-to-door survey to find out the spiritual mindset of the people
3. Share the gospel and give out tracts and Bibles.

One of our goals was to get to the Russian towns. We were told, “It won’t be easy.” Hiking wasn’t an option, and traveling by helicopter was too expensive. Instead, we rented a rubber Zodiac boat. “Wow, what an adventure this is going to be!” Phil shouted as we sped off toward Barentsburg, a Russian coal-mining town.

Darting through the drizzle and fog made me feel like I was in another spy movie—especially heading into Soviet territory. I was wearing my winter gear and a rain poncho. Phil wore warm clothes but had no rain protection. We arrived at Barentsburg after two hours at sea, and Phil was soaked.

A bold red communist sign—CCCP—and the prominent bust of Vladimir Lenin caught our attention as we walked into town. There was another large painting of the leader on a downtown building and a huge poster depicting strong young men and women at work.

I felt uneasy entering this town after hearing so many stories of the Soviet persecution of Christians. Our first impressions of the people we met were anything but harsh. Residents were out walking the streets. Some said “Hi,” others strutted straight ahead, a number of them wearing fur hats.

Phil’s voice broke my gaze, “Errol, if I don’t change into some dry clothes right away, I will get pneumonia. I’m freezing!”

“Oh Lord,” I prayed, “help us find a place for Phil to change.”

Then we spotted it—the Russian Consulate. Walking in, we knew what we would ask—Is it okay to walk around the town? Is it alright to take pictures? And then we’d ask to see Alexandr. Phil had met this young Russian at the Longyearbyen Airport. After briefly conversing, Phil discovered Alexandr was the Consulate official in Barentsburg. The night before this trip, Phil and I felt unanimous in prayer that we should visit Alexandr and offer him a Bible as a gift. Sure enough, he was there. Alexandr was a studious-looking young man, about six feet tall, dressed in a simple grey suit and he spoke perfect English.

Phil explained how we had come in a boat. Alexandr didn't seem to understand at first and looked quite serious. My first thought was, "He's upset we've come!" But he soon caught onto what we were saying and broke into a smile, "I'm glad you have come."

"Do you have a place where I could change out of my wet clothes?" Phil asked.

Alexandr led Phil to a room adjacent to the lounge. The consulate appeared relatively new and well-built. On the back wall hung another large picture of Lenin. Alexandr and I continued to talk in the hall, and an older man walked by, motioning for us to go into another room and sit down.

Alexandr began asking questions, and he appeared relaxed and friendly. "What kinds of work does your mission do?" he asked. "One branch of our ministry is with refugees," I answered. We try to show them kindness and help them fit into a new culture."

"Do you help prostitutes, drug addicts, and people like that?"

"Yes."

"Does it work?"

"Yes, it does. We've seen many people helped."

"Oh, is that so?"

"How did your work go in Longyearbyen?"

"It went well. We asked people what they thought about God. Then if they were interested, we would share with them what God has done in our lives."

Then, appearing genuine, he asked, "What has God done in your life?"

By this time, Phil had returned. I'd had some practice sharing my testimony over the past few days in Longyearbyen, and I truly felt the presence of God in the room.

"I was brought up in the church but never knew God. I even doubted His existence. However, when I was 17 years old, I had a deep stirring in my heart and felt there must be more to life than just living. Do you ever have those stirrings?" I asked Alexandr.

"Yes," he said.

I continued, "At one point, I cried out to God, 'If you exist, show me yourself'—and He did. He didn't come in the form of a bright light, but I realized that Jesus Christ deserved first place in my life. I also realized

Jesus died on the cross for my sins. After I opened my heart to Jesus, truths from the Bible became real to me. The Bible is an extraordinary book. It was written over a period of 1,500 years by over 40 different authors, and it should be the most mixed-up book in the world, but the fact is, it is harmonious from one end to the other."

"I have read some of the Bible," Alexandr said. 'Genesis, Exodus, but I got stuck in Leviticus."

Thankful for my Bible School training, I replied, "If you want to study more for yourself, match Leviticus with the New Testament book of Hebrews. They go together. The Old Testament sacrifices point to Jesus Christ, who became our perfect sacrifice."

"Do you have an English Bible you could give me?" Alexandr asked. I reached into the inner pocket of my winter jacket and pulled out a Russian New Testament. "We had wanted to give you this as a gift."

"Thank you, but do you have an English one? I'd like to study in English too."

Phil pulled out his New Testament with an apology, "It's wet." I then pulled out my personal Bible. It had Joyce's name in it, but I felt honored that he asked and gladly handed it over.

"Thank you for sharing all this with me," he said. "Thanks for listening."

"No, thanks for telling." Alexandr smiled. As we headed out the door to leave, Alexandr shouted, "Hey, wait."

He handed us two booklets. "I'm not a missionary for communism, but we need to understand each other better."

"Sure, we'll read them," I replied. "Even a husband and wife need to learn how best to communicate, how much more countries that are far apart."

He laughed and said, "Yes!"

As Phil and I walked back to the Zodiac, we heard a shout. We saw three men standing on the porch of a large blue house, motioning for us to come.

As we reached the porch, a police car drove by, and the men darted behind the door. They didn't want to be seen talking to foreigners even though things were becoming more open now in the Soviet Union, which actually collapsed, being then replaced June 12, 1990 by the modern day Russia.

The men seemed excited we were there and one knew a few English words. We knew no Russian, though Phil had a Russian/English dictionary.

The men seemed starved for contact with outsiders. They also wanted to trade with us. Sadly, we had nothing to offer except the Russian Bibles, which they refused. But as Phil and I were about to leave an hour later, they pulled things out of their drawers as gifts—a Russian fur hat for me, a multi-piece Matryoshka doll for Phil. I felt I should give them my watch and the Bibles, which they eventually received.

By the time we got down to the Zodiac, the low tide had beached it. I took off my shoes and socks and waded into the arctic water, struggling to get the boat water born. Just then, our three new friends showed up to help us—and off we went—into the grey mist.

After an hour, we pulled up to Coals Bay, a small mining outpost. At first I hesitated, wondering if I was ready for another encounter. Phil said, "Let's go."

Once again, people were friendly and wanted to trade with us. At the edge of the settlement, we found an abandoned factory building. We left our last two Russian Bibles there, praying the right people would find them.

Before heading back out to sea, we picked up some rocks from the beach. These were for the Stones of the Nations display at YWAM's University of the Nations campus in Kona, Hawaii.[2]

We stopped once more on the way back to camp. We were so focused and tense during our visit to the two Russian towns that we hadn't eaten in twelve hours. On a sheltered, rocky beach, we now took time to cook dinner, eat, and relax.

As we sat there on the beach unwinding, we took in the glories of the high cliffs teeming with fluttering birds. I marveled that we had just experienced a touch of the Soviet Union, a place of my family's roots. My Mennonite grandparents grew up in Russia and fled to Canada before the 1917 revolution.

By 1 a.m. we reached our campsite. After unloading gear, we returned the rented Zodiac and walked five kilometers back to our tent. By now it was 3 a.m. The polar sun, still high in the sky, illuminated the

2 www.uofnkona.edu

tent but we were exhausted and slept the minute we lay down. We awakened to a frigid wind howling across the ocean. If we had waited a day, we wouldn't have been able to cross the stormy waters in the Zodiac!

Phil Gazley and I on a remote beach with the Zodiac, and with my prized Russian fur hat called a 'Ushanka'

Chapter 11

Going Where God Leads

After Svalbard, our ministry and family life sped up like a whirlwind. I continued as temporary director of YWAM Edmonton while planning new ministry initiatives for Greenland. That November, our son Anthony was born. Joyce and I stood in awe beholding our fourth precious child. Our family was complete.

The following spring we launched our third successful DTS in Greenland. We returned home after five months and I resigned from YWAM Alberta responsibilities so I could focus fully on Greenland. I am forever grateful to God for a wife who understood His call on my life and was willing to lay aside her own comforts to support that call, no more so than when on one sunny September afternoon while she and I sat in our backyard on lawnchairs in Canada, we decided to make a move to Greenland. Amazingly, Joyce never once, in all the years, ever complained about the winter darkness, the winter blizzards, or the winter cold of Greenland.

My mind was in overdrive and I blurted, "It's time for me to get cracking if we're going to be ready for our move to Greenland early in the new year. We need to find long-term renters for the house, passports updated, flights booked, finances raised." Joyce listened patiently, having heard this kind of rambling from me before.

"Besides that, we need to put a crate together with some of our belongings."

Joyce nodded in agreement. "We'll need a lot of homeschooling books for the kids," she added, "plus their bikes, snow sleighs, and lots of winter clothes and boots."

"Yeah, and let's take our cross-country skis." Pausing for a moment of reflection, I continued, "And seeing as we are sending a crate anyway, let's fill any empty spaces with stuff like toilet paper and cans of food. They are a fraction of the cost here in Edmonton compared to Arctic prices."

"And gifts too!" Joyce added.

It was minus 40 degrees on the day in February 1990 when we packed up our car with our four children and drove out of Edmonton. We'd never experienced temperatures that low in all the winters we lived on the Greenland coast. Because the YWAM King's Kids ministry was being pioneered in Greenland, we were making a long drive to a King's Kids conference in New Jersey U.S.A. After the conference, we left our car at the YWAM base in Ontario and flew to what now felt like home in Sisimiut, just north of the Arctic Circle.

We moved back into the upstairs rooms of the Mission House and spent the winters of '90 and '91 there, continuing ministry as an international team. Greenlanders Brian and Angaju Wind, who had been students in the '89 DTS, were a big help in ministry preparations for the coming year.

Brian served as our Greenlandic language teacher. He told us, "I learned a lot of English from watching Kung Fu movies growing up." I chuckled at this unlikely source for learning, but Brian clearly had a gift for language. As he hung around us English speakers his ability improved to the point that he became a good interpreter. I wished I was half as good at learning Greenlandic!

Outside of Greenland, I've been asked many times, "Did you learn to speak the Greenlandic language?" My standard answer is, "Yes, of course. One hundred percent of what I know, ha." My Greenlandic friends were all so patient and encouraging in the process of my learning. Their faces would light up with delight at any new words and phrases I'd speak out, especially in the early days.

It takes humility on the part of a missionary to learn a new language. There is plenty of opportunity to feel awkward while practicing new phrases in the community—you just have to go for it by faith. On the other hand, I've been awed at the humility of my Greenlandic friends' willingness to learn new things from foreign missionaries who barely know their language or culture.

The summer of 1991 marked eight years since I'd first come to Greenland. In those years we had completed five Discipleship Training Schools, fourteen outreaches, and the launch of [3]King's Kids. Most importantly, many Greenlanders had been born again through the ministry.

My vision for Greenland continued strong—*doing my part to see disciples of Jesus serving in all regions of the country*—but I was weary and in need of spiritual refreshing. I had now been in full-time ministry for fifteen years.

At that time, our mission was encouraging YWAM leaders from all over the world to attend a three-month Leadership Training School in Kona, Hawaii. Joyce and I prayed about it and decided to take a sabbatical time to do the school. It began in January of '92. Amalie Olsen Møller, a close family friend from Sisimiut who'd helped Joyce launch King's Kids, also came along. She liked Kona's tropical flowers and the spiritual atmosphere on the base, but the area's resident cockroaches not so much. We don't have insects like that in Greenland.

* * *

Large snowflakes, illuminated against the black sky of the early morning were falling gently when I arrived back in Greenland later that year. A cheer of welcome from my Greenlandic friends went up the moment I

---

3 Mission Statement of King's Kids International: To lead children, youth, and families in knowing God, bringing Him joy, and together making Him and His Kingdom known - www.kki.global

appeared at the railing of our passenger ship as it pulled into Qaqortoq, South Greenland. What an encouraging feeling that gave me! Sadly, it would be quite a different feeling leaving the harbor eight months later.

Qaqortoq was the town where some of our DTS students back in 1987 didn't feel like handing out gospel magazines. Now a team made up of mostly former DTS students was here for church planting. I was excited to be with them.

Ever since I started the DTS program in Greenland, I was hoping for the emergence of new DTS leaders to take my place. However, no one felt called, and some of the staff were moving on to other ministries. When I asked Kaali to lead the next school, he said to me, "I don't want to have to deal with interpretation all the time, which is required for these international schools. I would rather work in my own language."

Kaali and Kattak, who were now married, decided to do church planting in Qaqortoq and invited Joyce and I to join them. We decided it was a perfect opportunity to support this young team and focus on language learning without all the pressures of organizing and leading DTS.

Kaali was a gifted young man in his late 20s. Earlier he had been Greenland's cross-country ski champion five years in a row. He was good at the dramas we'd been doing on outreach and was an engaging speaker and leader. Kattak is cheerful and warm. Someone you feel comfortable being around.

Soon after arriving, Kaali began telling me more about their vision. "Eroll, it is so good to have you here. We are all young, and we need a father."

Their plan was to plant a Pentecostal church supported by Kattak's home church in Norway. "We are going to partner with YWAM," Kattak said. "Our leaders in Norway are happy for this since YWAM is interdenominational."

Kaali continued telling me the great things God was doing over the past months.

"Monika, who came to the Lord through our DTS outreach in Nanortalik, was healed of tuberculosis. Another man received Christ and was healed of arthritis in his hands; a woman in town has been healed of gallstones, and another of a bad back. Others from town are calling on me to pray for deliverance from fear and ghosts in their houses."

"*Eroli, Guuti sulivoq* (Errol, God is working)."

"*Assa! Pissanganartoq*!" (Wow! Exciting!), I exclaimed.

On December 22, Joyce and the children arrived. It had been almost a month since we'd seen each other, but in the meantime, I'd rented a little blue house just down the steep hill from the church. I got things set up, including a Christmas tree with gifts under it that had come in a crate we'd sent from Canada.

One day Kaali spotted the empty crate outside our house. "Eroli, that crate would make a great baptismal tank! What do you think?"

"That's a great idea—go ahead!"

Soon Kaali recruited believers with the skills to fiberglass the crate. Within a short time it facilitated twenty-two baptisms.

Our family settled comfortably into life in Qaqortoq, including school for the children. By this time our kids were speaking Danish—the language most used in schools at the time. And then, to their delight, we got a fluffy white dog named Sinnatoq, meaning *Dream*.

* * *

The church in Qaqortoq was doing well, so much so that the team was aiming to plant more churches in southern Greenland. One target was a picturesque village about a two-hour speed boat trip from Qaqortoq. We'd been here before, and now Kaali and I were here again with a small team doing ministry in the home of a local Christian couple. I loved being the only foreigner among them, enjoying their company, and watching them minister effectively in their own language.

Later that sunny June day, I sat on a rock just beyond the village, praying and thinking. I noticed spring had come here a month earlier than in Sisimiut, which is much farther north. I thought about the people and ministry in South Greenland. Then suddenly I had a sense that we would soon leave here. It wasn't the first time this came over me. For some time, I felt strong pulls between leaving and staying, but as more weeks passed, I knew it was time to go. When I discussed with Kaali our plans to leave, he was not happy and said in English, "This is not from heaven."

Even harder was saying goodbye to Mati, a young man whose heart had opened to the Lord through the church plant ministry. He was a talented musician and spoke several languages including English. Early on we decided to meet twice a week and became friends. He would teach me Greenlandic, and I would lead him in Bible study. One day out of the blue he said, "I hope you guys don't leave from here too soon."

All of us had aching hearts when after being in Qaqortoq for eight months, we headed back to Sisimiut.

Chapter 12

A Touch of the Holy Spirit

We lived the next three years in Sisimiut. While it felt like home, the sadness I felt from disappointing Mati lingered. He called me several times from South Greenland expressing emotional pain even to the point of taking his own life. Sadly, at the time, I didn't possess the knowledge and skill to help much.

Then there was Kaali and Kattak. We'd been through so much together over seven years. They had been involved in four Discipleship Training Schools; we'd led outreaches together; they had visited us in Canada; I'd seen them grow in the Lord and ministry; we'd connected in so many ways, and I loved them as friends. But my relationship with Kaali had now become strained. A hardness seemed to have come over him, and slowly the church plant started falling apart and eventually his marriage. Many became stuck in the ice of their emotional pain, and it seemed to be spreading to others, including me. Over the years so many wonderful spiritual breakthroughs had taken place, and now this! I felt numb.

Amazingly, years later, I stumbled across a short paragraph from the intercession notes taken by the '89 DTS outreach team; those sentences shocked me. *"The reason so many fall is because of their soul wounds. Attention must be given to this in your ministry."* On that same outreach, in one of the meetings, Kaali himself had declared, "A soul healing center should be established." The fulfillment of the DTS's prayer and Kaali's declaration would eventually come, and with great power. Not a local healing center but a traveling healing ministry that would impact this very town multiple times, along with towns all over Greenland.

In the meantime, I can't say I was experiencing an abiding sense of love, joy, and peace. I was wrestling with some inner turmoil, along with the external challenge with language learning and finding meaningful ministry. But I carried on as best I could, praying, reading the Bible, and seeking God. Very slowly some breakthroughs started coming, one after the other.

A few months after arriving back to Sisimiut, a young woman named Bolette came to the Lord. However, her husband Lars Peter was angry about her becoming a believer and hated the Christian music she was playing in their home.

One day Lars Peter even went to see a *palasi* (priest) at the town's State Lutheran Church to complain about the Canadians who were influencing his wife. In response, the *palasi* called Zionsborg saying, "I want to have a talk with those Canadians." I decided to go see him. David, Sven's brother, agreed to come along.

As we walked into the church office, we were greeted by two priests. From a quick glance around the room, I noticed five simple chairs and a desk stacked with files. A picture of Queen Margareta of Denmark and her husband hung on a wall.

"What church are you with?" One *palasi* asked, directing his question to me.

"I'm with an interdenominational mission."

"You didn't answer my question."

"I was raised a Baptist." That seemed to be the answer he was after.

David spoke up in Greenlandic, explaining the difference about baptism expressed by Baptists, Pentecostals (David's background), and the Lutheran Church.

"Well, it's a problem when a wife and husband go in different directions, and bad things are being said about the State Church," the priest said.

"For several years we always took our discipleship school students to the Lutheran Church Sunday mornings," I responded.

That was one of Loren's exhortations to us in 1986 when Sven and I were discussing with him how to launch a DTS there. He said, "Attend the Lutheran Church as a DTS, and silently pray while you are sitting in the service." We did that on Sunday mornings through the lecture phase of the schools.

"What are your goals for the people?" I asked the men.

"We teach them the sacraments and church functions," one answered.

The other *palasi* expressed frustration. "Why don't you try being a priest in Greenland—there is so much paperwork!"

"We'd like to support you somehow," I said.

"Foreigners coming here should learn the language. How can they communicate without knowing the language?" He sounded perturbed.

Up until then, David had been translating for me. This time I replied, "*Utoqatserpunga, Kalaallisut oqaluppiasinnaainnginama. Kisi anni suli ilinniarpunga.*" (Excuse me, I can't speak much Greenlandic, but I'm learning).

The *palasis* seemed surprised but pleased. They spoke with David a bit more, and then we left. As we were walking away David said, "Errol, when you replied in Greenlandic, the Sisimiut *palasi*'s demeanor really changed. He invited us to visit him again, at his home, or in the office, but not to talk about religion."

Things changed in the heart of Lars Peter too. Seven months later, he was asked, "Are you ready to receive Jesus into your heart?"

He answered, "Without a doubt, I'm ready."

Soon after Lars' conversion he started attending the New Life Church (INO) with Bolette. They were living in Nuuk at the time.

Then something made him angry and he started drinking again. Bolette moved back to Sisimiut, but she kept praying for and pursuing her husband.

One day she called him and said, "Hey Lars, quit your job, get on the ship, and come back to Sisimiut. We are having special meetings here that might help you."

Lars Peter did just that. He quit his job, made the twenty-two-hour trip to Sisimiut, dropped off his bag, came over to Zionsborg, and sat down in the meeting which was already in progress. After a few minutes, the guest Bible teacher, Mareth Warren from Snohomish, Washington, gave an invitation to anyone who wanted prayer. Lars Peter responded.

"During the ministry time he fell over and cried for two hours," Bolette recalled. "During that time, he experienced an inner healing, and got up a changed man." One strong evidence of this change was Lars's decision to extend forgiveness to his abusive stepfather who was now living in a care facility. Lars said, "After forgiving my stepfather I experienced a love I never knew before, and I didn't fall back to my old life."

His old life had been filled with drinking, adultery, and rage. The hostility had been imparted to him from his stepfather, who himself was that kind of person. He despised and tormented Lars Peter because he wasn't his natural son. When he was six years old, the family decided to move. They all got into a speedboat ready to leave. But then Lars Peter's stepfather took him out of the boat, said, "You're not coming with us," and sped away. Lars Peter was left standing on the dock with nowhere to go.

"An elderly lady took me in," he recalled. "She was an alcoholic, and there were times of fear. But she was also kind. Two years later this kind stepmother was found dead in the snow, and my heart broke again. Next, I went to live with her daughter. Their home was like the home I was raised in, children cowering while adults drank, smoked, and shouted."

Sven-Olov baptized Lars Peter on the same day that I baptized our sixteen-year-old daughter, Tanya. Their going down under the water symbolized death to the old self, and being raised up out of the water symbolized their new life in Jesus. Bolette witnessed a supernatural evidence of new life in her husband. She said, "I could smell a sweet aroma after Lars Peter came up out of the water. A smell I'd never smelled before. It was something extraordinary."

Mareth Warren continued visiting us in Sisimiut with her ministry teams. She had been praying intensely for Greenland over a three-year span. Not only did Mareth minister spiritually, she recruited three work teams to help refurbish Zionsborg. Even my father got in on it through purchasing construction supplies and shipping them up. Sven-Olov, me, and these skilled volunteers worked together for weeks. Much was accomplished, including the replacement of the honey buckets with real flush toilets!

During that three-year season in Sisimiut, the summer of 1995 proved to be a significant ministry time in partnership with Sven-Olov. The King's Kids ministry was flourishing. In June, the Greenland team joined a larger King's Kids team in Denmark for outreach to the Ukraine. They were gone two weeks. While they were away, Sven and his family returned to Zionsborg after a seven-month furlough in their native Sweden.

I was delighted to have them home, and I had news. "Sven, there is a three-person team from a YWAM worship school in Kona, Hawaii, coming here for their outreach phase. Maybe they can join up with the returning King's Kids. They'll be landing in Kangerlussuaq in a few days, but they will need transport here to Sisimiut."

"I can pick them up in the speedboat. Why don't you come with me, Errol? It's a beautiful trip up the fjord."

We both loved the wilderness, and I jumped at the chance to go with my fun-loving friend. It was a whole different dynamic for us to be out there together bouncing along on the waves. I remembered one time when we were out at sea and caught some fish for lunch. We put them in a bucket of salt water and boiled them at the water's edge. Once it was done, the whole bucket was dumped onto a flat rock, and we were left with steaming pieces of delicious cod. As I was sitting there munching on the cod and taking in the rugged beauty of this seemingly endless wilderness, I exclaimed, "This is better than any restaurant I can imagine." Thereafter, Sven named that spot, "Errol's restaurant."

Kangerlussuaq sits at the end of the longest fjord in West Greenland—120 miles (190 km) long. The town is small, but it has largest airport in Greenland. It was first built during World War II as a strategic base for US fighter planes. Sisimiut is situated around a jut of this fjord and on a nice day is a 7 hour speed-boat ride away.

The team we picked up included a young man from England, a young woman from South Korea, and team leader Eleanor Rich from New Zealand.

By late July a large team had assembled in Zionsborg including more Greenlandic youth, the Ukraine team, and lots of guests for the Sunday evening service.

After worshipping together, a King's Kids performance, and testimonies from the Ukraine team, I began to wrap up the meeting. At the end, I simply said, "If anyone wants to come forward to pray for the Ukraine, or anything else, just come and gather around me here at the front."

As the Kona team led in worship and prayer, I knelt by the platform and started praying silently. After a few minutes I heard a strange noise behind me. I kept praying as the noise got louder. Upon cranking my head around, I was astonished to see twenty King's Kids on the floor behind me! The intensifying noise was a mix of laughter, weeping, and deep groans of anguished prayer. Laughter would turn to crying and crying to laughter and it went on. Some lay on the floor with their hands in the air worshipping God, while others sat on the platform holding their sides with laughter.

It was something I'd never witnessed before. I'd heard about a revival which had begun at the Airport Vineyard Church in Toronto in 1994. British newspapers referred to it as "The Toronto Blessing." This revival spread to many parts of the world, including Kona, where the worship team had just come from. I didn't know it, but they were fully expecting it to happen during their ministry time in Greenland. They had seen this blessing impart God's love, healing, and spiritual renewal everywhere they went.

The experience of that evening continued for hours. The Bible says, "Be not drunk with wine wherein is excess, but be filled with the Spirit." That's indeed what happened that night.

In those days we'd always have cake, snacks, coffee, and juice for the people after the evening service. The night of that outpouring all the goodies were left untouched. With a room full of teenagers, that is proof enough this night was miraculous!

Bolette, Lars Peter and Amalie were part of King's Kids staff at that time. Bolette said later, "Amalie and I were sitting next to each other when this all broke out. We looked at each other and began laughing too. We ended up laughing so hard we both fell on the floor and continued laughing and soaking in God's love. Soon after I returned home, a dark presence came out of my mouth—I felt I'd been delivered."

A year later, I was in another town and had opportunity to chat with one of the young girls who was in that meeting. She said, "You know, that experience really touched me. Sometimes I think back on it and it helps me in different situations. I felt God's presence so strongly and there was a deep working in my heart."

Then there was our twelve-year-old daughter Jayna. "Dad", she told me afterward, "I'd just prayed a few days before that unusual evening, and said, 'Lord, if you exist, show me yourself somehow.' The experience that evening was an answer to my prayer!"

Lars Peter and Bolette Jensen with daughter Naja—summer in Sisimiut.

Chapter 13

Spiritual Food for Greenland

Having lived in Edmonton, our children were used to long winters and life in the heavy snow. But Greenland gave them opportunities they never had back home—riding small boats among icebergs, fishing at sea, driving dogsleds, eating seal meat, and learning other Greenlandic ways, including one I hadn't expected.

One day, I received an official-looking letter from the Greenland government. Inside was a hunting license. I had not applied for one. It came automatically because the government now recognized us as long-term residents. In the Arctic, people have long depended on hunting and fishing for survival. Though the culture is changing, it's still quite natural for Greenlanders to hunt and fish for food.

As a kid in western Canada, I had hunted gophers and squirrels, and I'd dreamed of hunting big game. Joyce knew this, and under the Christmas tree that year was a surprise, a .22 caliber rifle. It was not big enough for reindeer, or musk oxen, but perfect for hunting Arctic hares.

One February day, I said to Tanya, "Hey, it looks like a great day for a hunting trip."

She glanced out the window and saw that the wind had died down. "Yes. Let's go!"

After packing a good lunch, hot drinks, and extra winter clothes, we harnessed up the seven excited sled-dogs and were off like a shot. If you weren't secure on that sled once you unchained it, you'd be left behind!

By this time, we both knew how to drive them. After several hours, Tanya and I reached a fjord at the bottom of a steep mountain pass. We crossed the thick ice on the fjord and secured the dogs. We seemed all alone in this wilderness of snow, but I knew there were big Arctic hares here. We hiked farther up to find one.

A few weeks later—on Easter morning—our family was seated around the table with a Greenlandic family we'd become close to over the years. Our relationship began soon after we met their daughter, Amalie, who was in her twenties. She'd become a believer while living in Denmark, and after returning home to Sisimiut, she started visiting Zionsborg. Her bubbly personality and strong faith made her a wonderful leader and interpreter for our King's Kids ministry.

Joyce had laid out all the favorites for Easter breakfast—fresh bread, cheese, yogurt, cold cuts, a special egg dish, and European coffee. But the best was yet to come. Part way through the meal, she went to the oven and pulled out the roasted Arctic hare that Tanya and I had brought home from our hunting trip.

When our guests saw it, their eyebrows lifted and they shouted, "*Assa* (wow)."

Amalie's mother said, "We loved eating these when we were children living farther up the fjord. But we haven't eaten one for a long time."

Food was key to helping our family bond with the Greenlandic people, but a bigger spiritual banquet was being prepared.

Sven-Olov and I were still meeting together regularly to talk and pray. One project we were all working toward was the INO* church conference Sven had volunteered to host in Sisimiut. In May, passenger ships from the north and south arrived carrying conference participants.

It was always a joy to get together for these conferences, especially after being isolated in remote towns during the long winter months.

During the conference week various leaders shared in teaching, preaching, and discussion. I spoke about visionary leadership from the book of Nehemiah. A new vision had been brewing in my heart and would be presented the next day.

The seed was planted from an outreach report given by Ha Nguyen after leading a YWAM team in East Greenland ten years earlier. He said, "Errol, as an outreach strategy we showed the Jesus film in English, with an interpreter. It was too long to show that way in one sitting, but it was still effective."

That two-hour movie on the life of Christ had been translated into more languages than any other film on earth, and I thought, "Why not Greenlandic!"

As the idea of a Jesus Film Translation Project got stronger, I ordered fifty copies with Danish subtitles. Since most Greenlanders understand at least some Danish, I was confident the video would have an impact, and it did. But my heart longed for them to hear the message in their mother tongue.

The day after I taught about vision, Brian Vaughn and Martin Epp, two representatives from the Jesus Film Project in Langley, BC, took the platform and told inspiring Jesus Film stories from around the world. They explained what it would take to translat the film into Greenlandic.

After hearing this report, everyone was enthused. We knew it would be lots of work, money, and unprecedented church unity to bring it to pass. But we were committed.

Soon after that I met with eight of the leaders from the conference at the Seamen's House Hotel to plan and discuss delegation of tasks for the Jesus Film Project translation.

"I could be the main contact person here in Greenland," volunteered John Østergaard Nielsen, a Danish pastor/missionary in Nuuk, "And I'll help find voice actors."

"This film will be very good for our people. I'll take on the translation task," Aqqalu Berthelsen said with a smile.

I was thrilled by their response, "Joyce and our family are returning to Canada soon, so from there I can do the fundraising," I responded.

All at once, Dr. Joe Bruce stood to his feet. "This project is the providence of God!" He said, "We of the International Mission Board of the Southern Baptist Convention will donate the first five thousand US dollars." I was astounded.

Two months earlier the phone had rang in Zionsborg. I answered, and on the other end was Dr. Joe Bruce who identified himself and his Southern Baptist affiliation, then said, "One of my colleagues and I would like to come up to Greenland to see what is going on for the gospel and how we can help. We are not coming to plant Baptist churches but to simply support a project that is already going on."

I said, "We are having a church leaders conference here in Sisimiut the week in May. It will be perfect timing for you to come, as we are going to be launching the Greenlandic Jesus Film Translation Project."

Dr. Bruce and his associate did come, and their enthusiasm and generosity were a huge boost. Another unexpected gesture of support came the next morning at the heliport where we were seeing off the conference guests. As we were waiting, another helicopter landed, and its passengers came walking through.

Sven-Olov perked up and declared, "Hey. There's Lars-Emil Johansen, the Premier of Greenland."

At once, our friend Martin Epp approached the Premier and told him about the translation project. Mr. Johansen looked surprised and pleased. "You mean to tell me that you are planning to translate a film into Greenlandic? I am very interested!" The Jesus Film Project had been launched, and we even had an encouraging word from the Premier.

Tanya and the dogs returning at the end of our hunting trip.

Chapter 14

Finishing the Jesus Film

The week following the conference, Joyce and I started sorting through our belongings. What were we going to carry back to Canada, what were we going to store in Zionsborg? And what were we going to sell?

We had finally made a firm decision to move back, and it had been just as difficult as leaving South Greenland. During those days, I'd wake up in the morning with tormenting thoughts. Why must we leave? We're just getting to know the community and just starting to build up the church. I'd written in my diary, "Is there another way?" Besides all that, there was something else in the back of my mind, the hunting license. Now I won't be able to use it!

One evening, in January, we'd had a little family time with all four children. "Where do you want to live?" I asked. "I'd like each of you to share your feelings. Should we stay here in Sisimiut or go to Canada?"

> **Jayna** (13) was first, "I want to stay in Greenland, except for summer, and I want a different school arrangement."
> **Anthony** (7) was next, "We must go back to Canada or I'll stay in my bed!"
> **Angela,** (8) "We must go back to Canada but I want snow too."
> **Tanya** (16) chimed in at the end. "Mom and Dad should stay in Greenland but I really want to take my grade 12 in Canada."
> **Joyce** said, "I'm open either way."

Hearing Joyce say that warmed my soul, as that standard of openness to the Lord was what I tried to live by.

I asked the Lord to confirm our decision by his Word, and he did. Exactly three months later I was reading the story of Jesus and the disciples getting into the boat and "crossing over to the other side." As hard as it was to pull out, I knew in my heart that's what we needed to do—cross back over to Canada. I received another scripture (Jeremiah 29: 4–7) three times in a row. I'd come across it myself first and then two others gave it to me, not at all knowing what it would mean to me.

The scripture carried the idea of being pulled between two different locations, building a house, planting a garden, eating its fruit, marrying off children, having grandchildren, and continuing to pray for the place not your home of origin (Greenland). Looking back, every part of that has come to pass, plus much more than I could have imagined.

We left the great island on July 2, 1996 but Greenland did not leave us. About ten days after arriving at my parents' place in Vancouver, BC, the Greenlandic King's Kids team arrived to perform and share in the Vancouver and Seattle area. For several of the young people it was the first time seeing trees.

I was also carrying a new vision for Greenland inside of me—the Greenlandic Jesus Film Translation Project. But first we had to find a place to live. We settled in Kelowna, BC, where Joyce's parents lived. There was a YWAM base nearby, along with the Western Canada Director, Paul Martinson, who had been so supportive of the Greenland vision from day one.

Now it was time to raise funds for the film. I started calling churches, "Could I please speak to your missions committee leader, I have a project you might be interested in supporting."

Every church I called said their missions budget was topped up, and one pastor told me, "I'm trying to protect my people from people like you." Not too encouraging.

A year after moving into our house in Kelowna, I was back in the air, on my way to Greenland.

The yearly INO conference was already in session when I arrived at Zionsborg. There were hugs and warm greetings and I felt so at home.

It had been sixteen months since the conference where we'd shared the Jesus film vision. I had committed to raising the $40,000 for the project and, despite the slow start in Kelowna, all the funds had come in.

Aqqalu Berthelsen, with help from a friend, had also fulfilled his part with the translation of the entire two-hour film.

The only area still lacking was the need for a few more voice actors. Aqqalu made a plea during one of the conference sessions, and Lars Peter, Bolette, and Amaile all volunteered. Before the first recording session began in Nuuk, all the spots were filled by talented Greenlandic believers.

The technicians were to arrive in Nuuk in the afternoon, but their flight was aborted in Ottawa. At first I felt panic, but then remembered a word I'd heard, "It is often during the recording that prayer is most needed." The next day Richard and Becky, the technicians, arrived safely in Nuuk. This couple was not new to travel or recording; Richard had done thirty languages so far. "Since I was a young boy, I have had a desire to visit Greenland. I'm thrilled to be here," he said.

The ten-day recording schedule would be intense. Some twenty Greenlanders lent their voices and talents to replace the English voices on the film. For example, the Apostle Peter's voice would take about three hours (Lars Peter would play that part). The narrator recordings would take five to ten hours. An elderly Greenlandic man who was a famous radio voice in Greenland accepted that part.

The process involved long days of tedious recording sentence by sentence, and sometimes word by word. The emotions had to be right, the timing had to be right, the volume had to be right. At times one take was all that was needed; on other more complicated parts it could take thirty minutes to get one sentence right.

The Greenlandic language structure is much different than English. The hard part was getting the lip-synch as close as we could. One day Aqqalu explained to us, "Notice, for example, how many syllables the English word 'teach-er' has—two."

"The Greenlandic word for teacher, *i-li-ni-ar-tsi-tsi-soq*, has *seven*. So what do you do? You find another word to replace teacher if you can. In this case we used the word *a-jor-qi*, meaning 'a priest's helper.' That word has only three syllables."[4]

One day my Danish missionary friend John said, "Errol, let's go to Katuaq, the Culture House, and see what they say about showing the film there." The Culture House was a brand-new multi-purpose auditorium with ability to host full-feature movies. It was the first official theater in Greenland and it had just opened—perfect timing for the Jesus film!

As we talked the director said, "I think about 6,000 potential viewers out of Nuuk's population of 13,000 will want to see this film. It is the first in Greenlandic, and they are interested in Bible stories." He went on, "Maybe we can file through all the school students, and then all from the seniors home."

We discussed whether we should show the film with a 16mm projector or invest in an expensive 35mm print. We decided to go all out with the 35mm. *That means more fundraising for me*, I thought to myself. *I want the film to have maximum impact.*A few days later I was sitting in the radio station with Aqqalu. We were being interviewed by a Greenlandic journalist about the film. The interview was broadcast the following Sunday afternoon all over Greenland, and it had piqued a lot of interest, including the local TV station which asked to show the film on national television. We didn't want that to happen just yet. First, we wanted to use the film in a more direct evangelistic format. Once that was done, yes, we would broadcast it over the whole country.The film was nearly complete in October and we arranged for a showing that evening. We wanted those present to advise us of any mistakes they noticed. About thirty Greenlanders were present.

---

4 Jesus, of course, was not just a "priest's helper" in the earthly sense. He is our *great high priest* (Hebrews 4:14). However, during his ministry on earth Jesus humbled himself and said, "I only do what I see my Father doing." (John 5:19), and, "The Son of Man came not to be served, but to serve…" (Matthew 20:28)

As the film began, tears came to my eyes. I watched Greenlanders listening intently. One of our former DTS students came up to me. "Oh, the film is just perfect. If they were available, I'd buy a video right now and give it to my parents."

A week later, I was on the way back to Canada. The Greenland trip was an incredible success. Everything we'd planned was fulfilled. And there had been something else going on behind the scenes—a lot of counseling. It seemed the trip was almost as much a pastoral visit as it was about the Jesus Film project. Many were hurting and had sought me out to talk. In a few years, myself and many others would be better equipped with biblical counseling skills. The way would be paved by The Jesus Film.

Some of the Greenlandic voice actors observing their work on the Jesus film. Left to right: Bolette, Dea, Amalie, Lars Peter, Kristian

Chapter 15

Historic Premiere

Seven months later, everything had come together for the film's premiere. I took off for Nuuk accompanied by Paul Martinson and three other mission leaders. As part of the outreach, we were taught by two of the Jesus Film Project staff how to use the film effectively, how to lead a person to Christ using a Greenlandic gospel tract, and how to follow up with discipleship.

John and Aqqalu greeted us with big smiles as we came through the security doors of the airport carrying 35mm prints of the Jesus film in two large metal containers—one weighing 43 pounds and the other 37 pounds. The film had been completed with some last-minute corrections at the Florida studio. The next morning, we dropped it off at the Katuaq Culture House.

Meanwhile, the Southern Baptists continued their active support. Two of their European representatives joined us for the premiere. On the first day we met one of the men who told me, "I've emailed our prayer hotline to pray for this outreach. At any given time, there could be 200,000 people praying for this."

"That's amazing," I said, feeling overwhelmed with gratitude.

"That's not all," Tim said. "My home church in the States has 4,500 members. The pastor announced this project from the pulpit and called for prayer. He asked if there were some who would like to pray and fast for Greenland over the weekend, and 450 said they would do so."

Then he asked me, "How are you doing financially?"

"I borrowed $20,000 for this launching."

"Let's see what we can do," Tim replied. An hour later he came back with his notebook computer showing me an email from headquarters. It said, "I think we can find $10,000 USD." And they did. The whole loan balance was met over the next few months.

Many individuals contributed help, prayers, and donations to bring us to this point. One YWAM group in Holland felt led to pray, "Let's believe that for every Guilder (Dutch currency) we donate, one Greenlandic soul will come into the kingdom." Two women took it as a personal challenge and raised $10,000 through Blue Mountain Baptist Church in Canada. Another woman from Canada flew all the way to Greenland to pray for the success of the Jesus Film outreach.

On May 24, exactly two years from when the vision was shared at the INO conference in Sisimiut, the film premiered in Nuuk at the Katuaq Culture House. Martin Epp, an associate of Inspirational Films introduced it. Then Karl Kristian Olsen, Greenland's director of Culture, Education and Religion at the time, declared: "This is very important for our people's language and spirituality."

We from industrialized countries, where thousands of movies are screened each year, can't begin to grasp the experience of seeing a movie in your own mother tongue for the first time. This was no ordinary film. Its message had a profound effect. When the people came streaming out of the theater after the showing, their faces appeared sober and thoughtful. Many filled out the response card they had been handed when they entered. Over the next three days, the film was shown nine times to a total of 553 people. Out of this number 50 percent said they prayed the salvation prayer at the end of the film, and 145 people provided contact information for a follow-up visit.

I had dreamed of having 5,000 people see the film in that first week. Later John said to Aqqalu, "I'm sure glad Errol's vision of 5,000 didn't take place. If it had, and the same percentage responded, we would have been overwhelmed with follow up."

In the weeks that followed, the film's outreach swept across Greenland like a warm wind melting many hearts.

Bjarne Jensen, Danish missionary to Ilulissat, wrote an article for the local newspaper about the Jesus Film, and it triggered what he described as a fantastic response: "Altogether 124 saw it, and as they left the building many had tears in their eyes. For the last three days people have been coming in streams to get a video. Most of the people in Ilulissat are talking about Jesus and the film, and we are getting calls from nearby villages too."

Aqqalu reported from Maniitsoq: "We showed the film in the public house and so many people came we had to lock the doors because of fire regulations. Every chair we could find was occupied. Many are now asking for videos, and the schools here are using them almost every day for some classes. Many schoolkids love to see *Jesus*!"

John Østergaard wrote from Nuuk: "It was so fantastic to see how people crowded to get a seat in the *Forsamlingshuset* (gathering house). A total of 500 people in two days, this was far more than we had expected. We have now been sharing the follow-up addresses among the believers."

When I went back to Sisimiut the following March, I brought 500 copies of the film. *Jesus* was shown three times in the hall near Zionsborg, and half of the 300 who saw it prayed the salvation prayer at the end. We had placed attractive posters around town, first advertising the movie showings and then the video sales. One day I felt a prompt from the Lord to go outside and sell them. At minus 20 degrees Celcius it was bone-chilling to stand for hours at a time, but the videos sold fast—five to ten each hour. I had set up a table beside the bus stop, and later near the town grocery store. In eight days I sold 225 videos and I had the joy of meeting dozens of people on the street.

One morning Lars Peter was with me at the table when a woman came up and told us, "I was feeling sick and called out, 'Who can help me?' I then lay down on the couch and fell asleep. I had a dream and saw the big yellow mission house (Zionsborg)—and heard the words, 'Someone at that house can help you.' I have never visited the house before." After hearing her story Lars encouraged her, "Come and visit us anytime."

An encouraging report for me personally was via email from Gudrun Toldam in Denmark. It read:

[[ex]]Dear Errol,

Dan and I just arrived back from the Greenland Mission Conference (INO) in Ilulissat. I would like to tell you how excited I am after having listened to the stories about how the Jesus Film has been used in Greenland ... It has filled many community houses already and many of the small villages have seen the film. One person buys it, and the whole village is invited to see the film in their house... I know the vision came from the Lord, and that it was Aqqalu and John and others who did a lot of hard work—but it is also a fact that if you hadn't been there and if you hadn't been obedient to God's voice, there wouldn't have been a Jesus Film in Greenlandic today."[[/ex]]

Gudrun's email touched me like a hug from the Lord. After moving out of Greenland in '96, I was feeling so low that I questioned my own usefulness to God. Old heart issues had re-surfaced, trying to convince me I had no gifts or talents to offer anyone.

After the success of the Jesus film project, I could have considered my work in Greenland done. But I had no release at all to quit. I just couldn't. I continued doing what lined up with my original vision—learning more Greenlandic, teaching on missions in the local DTS, and prayerfully pondering what God had next for Greenland. I'd soon find out the success of the Jesus Film Project was just the beginning of a much larger spiritual breakthrough, not only for Greenland, but for me. If I'd quit missions, I may have missed it all.

Jonathan Motzfeldt, long-time Premier of Greenland, holding a copy of the Jesus Film in Greenlandic. John Østergaard Nielsen (L); Aqqalu Berthelsen (R)

Chapter 16

Arctic Pilots for Christ

THOUGH OUR FAMILY was content to be home in Canada, my heart kept being tugged back to Greenland. The Jesus Film was a huge step forward, but there were still thousands more wounded hearts who needed to be touched by His healing grace. I didn't know yet how that would happen, but the Lord was preparing the way.

Early in 2001 David Åsblom called to ask if we could fill in for him and Jeanette at Zionsborg so they could take a much needed break. I decided to go up for a visit before making a commitment. I stayed in Greenland long enough to attend the annual INO conference in Nuuk. Church leaders were excited about the success of the Jesus Film, and everyone recognized the need for discipling new converts. Some suggested DTS could be an answer. I did a pitch for reviving the school but got no firm commitments for assistance or students.

I told one leader afterward, "The more I talk about starting up DTS again, the more uneasy I feel. What I am hearing from the people in the conference is a desire for teaching brought to them from town to town.

That way many more could benefit from it—and without having to give up homes and jobs. I'd appreciate your prayers." My friend soon called together a group of Greenlandic leaders to lay their hands on me and pray.

I returned to Kelowna with a lot to pray about and Joyce was eager to hear about it. As we were doing the dishes together one evening she asked, "What are you thinking about the invitation from David and Jeannette and about doing another DTS there?"

"I don't have clear guidance yet about Zionsborg, but I don't think we are going to run a DTS. I sense we need to be teaching from town to town—and it'll be something to do with counseling."

A few weeks after that conversation I got a phone call that provided the answer I had been seeking, and more.

A friendly male voice said, "Hello, this is Clair Schnupp. Some friends gave me your name after they heard me share my interest in Greenland. My wife Clara and I have been ministering among the Cree nation and other indigenous peoples of North America for forty years."

As we talked, I felt an instant connection with this man because of our shared concerns about the depression, suicide, alcoholism, and domestic abuse among these people groups. Clair and his wife Clara were now working in Northwestern Ontario where they developed a Biblical counselors training course to teach First Nations and Inuit believers to become biblical counselors in their own villages.

"People come to them with problems, they help process their emotions, lead them to Christ, and this in turn is contributing to church growth," Clair said.

I can't believe what I'm hearing, I thought. *This is what we need in Greenland*!

Clair continued, "We had been involved in youth ministry for years and then family counseling. No matter how much the people liked what we taught they couldn't get it to work in their lives because of deep emotional wounds that kept pulling them back to relational flare-ups and drinking. We have found that a believer can't grow spiritually with unhealed soul wounds."

"That's what we've seen in Greenland too."

"What kind of planes normally land up there?" Clair asked.

"Up until last year Sisimiut had only a helicopter pad. The same is true for most towns. But now several towns have air strips that can handle Dash 7s (turboprop commuter planes)."

"That will be fine for my airplane."

"You mean you're a bush pilot too?"

Clair laughed. "Yes, I can fly. Clara and I, and our secretary Dorcas, would like to visit towns in Greenland and introduce the course. If it sounds to you like our ministry could be a help in Greenland, would you mind setting up an itinerary?

"Yes! Clair, it sounds like this training is exactly what we need in Greenland."

That phone call turned into a twelve-year ministry that opened my eyes, put new skills in my hands, took me places I never dreamed, but most importantly, brought salvation, healing, deliverance, and hope to many in Greenland and other nations too.

After telling Joyce about the call, she said, "God's timing is amazing. Those theaters opened just in time for the Jesus Film showings. And now there are new airstrips just in time for Clair's airplane."

After packing up and renting out our house that fall, our 14-year-old daughter Angela and I drove 1400 miles (2300 km) to Dryden, Ontario to meet the Schnupps and fly with them to Greenland. Joyce and Anthony would follow in a couple of weeks. Meanwhile, Tanya was on her way to serve in Uganda and Jayna was completing her University of the Nations degree in Texas.

The Schnupps' Northern Youth Programs center reminded me of some of our rural YWAM bases. Situated on open grassy property between trees and a lake, it had an office building and a separate lodge with a kitchen, dining area, and dorm-style rooms. Like YWAM, they had volunteer staff.

The surprise for us was that the Schnupps and their volunteers were conservative Pennsylvanian Mennonites. The women wore long, simple dresses, with their hair pulled back under a small black head covering. Although I was raised in a Baptist church and my roots are Mennonite, I had never seen this before.

Many Pennsylvanian Mennonites describe their simple, godly lifestyle as "plain." Outsiders see their ways and sometimes say these people are out of touch with the real world. I found out nothing could be further from the truth. Clair had earned a PhD to facilitate counseling work and was one of the most experienced private pilots in Canada. Clara and their five daughters were also licensed pilots. This couple were among the most hardcore, in-the-thick-of-it missionaries I'd ever met. They'd faced the dark souls of thousands with love, compassion, faith, and skill. They'd eat anything, sleep anywhere, and fly anywhere—well, almost.

Clara confessed she had a fear of flying over open water. She said, "Clair, if we are going to take on Greenland, that means flying over open water, and that means you need to get us a better airplane."

"One of the best planes for Arctic regions would be the Cheyenne Piper because it has a turboprop engine," Clair told me, "The colder it is outside, the better that engine likes it. It's ten times safer than the gas engine bush planes." But to make the switch to that airplane Clair had to take Instrument Flight Rules (IFR) training. For an experienced bush pilot to switch from Visual Flight Rules (VFR) to Instrument Flight Rules is extremely challenging. Most bush pilots can't make the change. Clair said, "All my classmates quit, and I was tempted to quit too. But I had a holy calling and I felt like I couldn't live with myself if I bailed." Clair did receive his IFR certification. They could now fly over the Davis Strait to Greenland with a lot more safety in their newly purchased Piper Cheyenne.

When I first met the Schnupps they were in their mid-60s, and by that time Clara had been suffering from diabetes for about three years. Her doctor wanted her on medication but Clara said, "I'd like to see what I can do with exercise and diet." She took it seriously and thus avoided medication. I remember her praying at mealtimes, "Lord, help me eat right." Besides being a woman of faith, I found her a most gracious and appreciative person. She had a way of seeing and affirming the good around her.

Angela and I were now about to fly with this couple for the first time. At the appointed hour Clara pulled up to the lodge in a large green van and told us we had to be on our way. Unlike driving a car, flying a plane meant you had precise protocols to follow. When it was time to go, we had to go.

When we arrived at the hangar, Clair was checking over the plane. While we were loading, Clara said, "You don't look like you are dressed warm enough for the North."

Before I could reply, Clair answered for me, "He's been going to Greenland for nineteen years. He knows what it's like."

But I didn't know what it was like traveling in a small non-commercial plane. They are not as well insulated as the commercial planes we were used to. Even though it was October and not a cold day, Clair and Clara wore huge parkas with fur-lined hoods. Angela and I were wearing light jackets. After that flight, I always wore warm clothes when flying with Clair, especially in the Canadian Arctic which is much colder than Greenland's coast.

After three hours we stopped in La Grande, Quebec, for fuel and then landed in Iqaluit, Nunuavut, Canada, where we stayed for the night. It was always great to catch up with Pastor Wayne and Linda Moore, and once again I had a new team to introduce. Except this time, I was more part of Clair's team as a helper and student.

It had been a long day, but before we could sleep we had to "put the plane to bed"—that meant putting on the wing covers, tying the plane down in case of strong winds, blocking the tires, and plugging in the engine heaters if it was freezing. As the pilot, Clair had other tasks too.

Early the next morning we crossed the Davis Strait and landed in Sisimiut. After landing something took place that I'd never witnessed in all the years of entering the country. We were required to put our luggage through a scanner and several policemen met us with solemn faces asking to see our passports. One who knew me said, "Make sure you keep your passports with you at all times while in Greenland."

"What?! I'd never even once been asked for my passport before in all the times I'd entered Greenland." I remarked once we were back in Zionsborg.

Later David Åsblom told us, "You guys caused some fear here as you circled around before landing. Some people thought it was going to be another terrorist attack by Osama bin Laden like happened on September 11 in America a few weeks ago."

Because the Sisimiut airport was so new, it was a novelty seeing airplanes flying in, and the Cheyenne may have been the first private plane to land there.

Our family was planning to stay in Sisimiut for six months, so Angela and I had brought extra supplies with us. Unloading them seemed to go on and on. At one point David overheard one of the airport workers remark, "How in the world could they carry all that stuff in that little airplane?"

"They're believers!" the other answered.

Yes, but the most valuable thing we brought was what Clair described as, "a pearl, one of a kind"—the Biblical Counseling Course.

Over the coming years we would present the course in sixteen towns across Greenland including Qaanaaq in the North, Ittoqqortoormiit in the East, and Nanortalik in the South. While in the air we faced fog, blizzards, raging winds, closed airports, and minus 50 degrees Celsius (-58° F) temperatures that once froze the end of my nose. Clair handled the dangers with skill matching the best bush pilots of the Arctic. As we flew along Greenland's rugged coastline, he told me, "I'm a fearful pilot, that's why we're still alive." In other words, he knew what he could handle but wouldn't take chances.

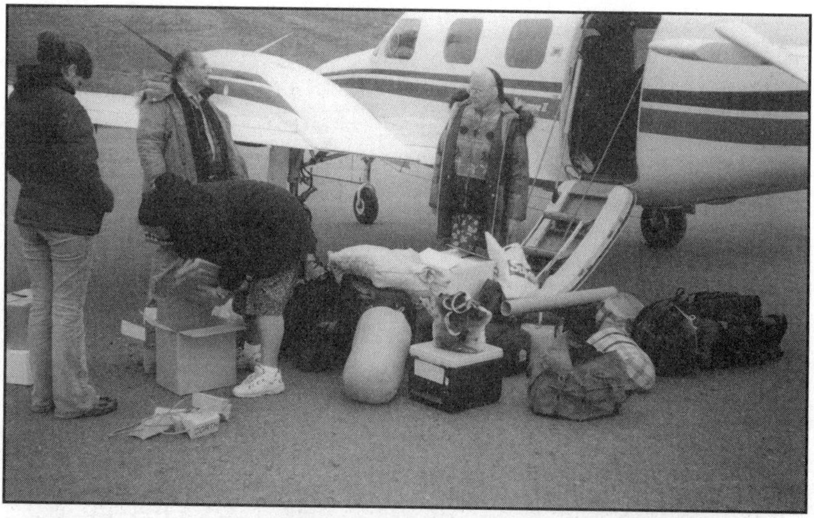

Our first historic trip together in the Cheyenne II. There would be over 30 more trips to follow. We carried a lot of ministry materials. Left to right: Angela, Dorcas (Dr. Clair's faithful secretary), Clair and Clara

Chapter 17

Getting Beneath the Ice

On our first trip together in Greenland my job was to introduce the Schnupps. Their job was to introduce the Biblical Counselors Training Course in evening presentations in four towns on Greenland's west coast.

The people sat riveted by the teaching. I too sat absorbing every word, now certain this was the ministry we'd all been waiting for. Clair and Clara's presentation on "draining the pain" was a door of hope to Greenlanders.

It helped so many emotionally wounded people enter the abundant life of love, joy, and peace Jesus offers. I was especially touched by a call I received from Brian Wind in Maniitsoq. "I can't say enough about the teaching and counseling. My wife's anger towards her father is gone and her outlook is so different. My anxiety is gone too. I think everyone who received this counsel was affected in a positive way."

I received similar responses from the other towns, and this was just the introductory trip with only two or three evenings of teaching.

Joyce, Angela, Anthony, and I spent our sixth Christmas and New Year in Greenland preparing for Clair and Clara's return in February. This time they planned to offer a six-day course in three towns.

Not long before they arrived, the four of us went to feed the sled dogs at the outskirts of town where they were being kept. It was minus 15 degrees Celsius with snow and a strong wind. I noticed one of the dogs acting strange. A moment later Anthony found out why.

"Look at this Dad," he exclaimed. He pointed to a hole dug in the snow. Inside was a litter of newborn puppies. The three on top were still alive, but the ones underneath were dead. Anthony and Angela scooped up the three live puppies and put them under their coats to keep warm. I then unchained the mother dog, and we took the little family back to Zionsborg. Several weeks later, they were all well and growing.

Just as our family had saved those puppies from cold, darkness, and death, so the Pain of the Heart ministry was comforting and saving many lives. The most tragic result of the nation's social ills was a high suicide rate.

One evening that subject came up while Joyce and I were meeting with an attractive young Inuit couple. The husband said, "There have been so many deaths and suicides in Sisimiut recently. People in town are saying to one another, 'Who will be next to die?'" The young wife and mother admitted she had attempted suicide several times.

The following Friday we were visiting with another young woman who shared a similar story. "A relative of ours sexually abused my sister and me for years. As a result, I became so hurt and confused, and sometimes thought I was going crazy. One night I decided to commit suicide. I stood on a chair, put a rope around my neck, and I was ready to hang myself. Then I looked down at my sister sleeping and realized how horrible it would be if she found me dead. So I didn't do it. The next day I went to school with a scarf around my neck to hide the marks from the tight rope."

"We're so sad for this pain in your life," I said. "Our counselor friends Clair and Clara say that sexual abuse and father wounds are two of the biggest contributors to suicide."

At this point, I had not yet been through the 10-week counselors training course. After Aaninnguaq left, I ran upstairs and grabbed the little booklet Clair and Clara had been giving out called, *When Trust is Lost: Healing for Victims of Sexual Abuse*, by Dr. Dan Allender.

The introduction said, "Sexual abuse is one of the few crimes that brings more shame to the victim than to the offender. It takes away a person's innocence and self-respect, and usually silences the victim so that help is difficult to find … Many victims feel alone, confused, depressed, and sometimes think they are going crazy."

Clair and Clara had witnessed this pain in Greenland, and I was both stunned and delighted when Clair sent an email to me that said, "We want to plan as many [Pain of the Heart workshops] as possible in the next three years. Your vision to saturate Greenland with these six-day workshops will fill a great need."

"We also are providing three staff so we can re-work each of the course manuals to an English version that could be translated into Greenlandic."

There was no doubt, God was intent on bringing healing to Greenland. In fact, He always had been, as is revealed in Isaiah 61:1, "The Spirit of the Lord is upon me, because he hath anointed me to preach the gospel to the poor; he hath sent me to heal the brokenhearted, to preach deliverance to the captives, and … to set at liberty them that are bruised." This scripture is applied to Jesus in Luke 4:18.

On February 1, the Schnupps and Dorcas landed back in Sisimiut. A fourth passenger was on the Cheyenne that day. Jayna was between university courses and came to join us. The next afternoon we flew to Nuuk where the first six-day, forty-hour workshop was run with fifteen students. Dr. Clair was on fire in his teaching—one time quite literally! As he spoke, he wasn't aware how close he was getting to a candle burning on a railing directly behind him. He felt a twinge of pain on his back and realized a hole had burned right through his sweater! At the same time, the fire of the Holy Spirit was starting to burn out the rubble that had collected in many troubled hearts.

One woman held up a fist-size-rock saying, "This week it was like a stone came out of my heart, and for the first time I can love my mother."

Our next class had even more students. At one point in his teaching Dr. Clair projected an iceberg diagram on the wall. This was especially appropriate because the town we were in was right beside the largest iceberg-producing glacier in the northern hemisphere. Dr. Clair reminded students that 90 percent of an iceberg is below the surface of the water.

"Just like the iceberg, it's easy to observe the outward problems in our lives like anger, depression, anxiety, fear, relationship problems and addiction problems. But the real sources of these troubles are under the surface, deep in our subconscious. We often don't recognize the influence they are having on our lives—these are the destructive heart beliefs and vows we made as children amidst traumatic times."

The elderly man sitting across the table from me had a soul wound from his father which was still affecting his life decades later. He said, "How can I forgive my father? It was 56 years ago, but I still feel anger toward him." His unresolved anger had horrifically affected his wife, children, and grandchildren.

Next Clara got up to teach. "You know, there is what we call big "A" abuse, and small "a" abuse. Big "A" abuse might be recognized as sexual abuse or witnessing the death of a parent as a young child. Small "a" abuse could simply be something as common as not being heard or understood—that's my story.

"When I was a little girl, I remember sitting around our large dinner table with my eleven siblings. My dad on one end of the table and my mother on the other end. Everyone was talking loudly and expressing their opinions. I had a thought I wanted to express on the subject, but when I spoke out my idea no one paid any attention. Everyone kept right on talking over me. I tried again and again but to no avail. I felt deep sadness and thought, *What I have to say is not important!* And that was the lie that became lodged in my heart. I followed that belief with a vow: '*I will never* try to express my ideas again!' This too became lodged in my heart."

Clara said after getting married, she eventually became deeply depressed. "It was supressed anger. Because I'd been pushing it down, I didn't even realize I was angry. Lots of people would call me to discuss *their* problems. I would listen but would never tell anyone *my* problems, and I rarely shared my opinions. I was a schoolteacher back then. I could stand up and teach lessons, but that was different from sharing my heart in daily life.

"Later when Clair and I were getting our master's degrees in counseling from Providence Theological Seminary I was in my small group. At one point our lab leader asked me, 'Clara, why do you never share with us?'

"And then it hit me—it all came up in my mind—the table, the rousing discussion, and the little girl who had believed a lie and made a vow. I cried and cried as I thought about how I had hurt my own daughters by not sharing my heart with them, and how my life had been affected in so many ways."

Then Clara said she realized how angry she was at Clair. "Because I wouldn't share how I really felt about things, resentment started building up in me. When I repented of the lie and vow, I chose to see myself differently. Sharing my thoughts more freely was hard at first, but I kept at it. Today I tell Clair exactly what I think, and because he also has been healed of his lies and vows, he is able to hear me—our relationship is so much better today."

Then Clair stood up and told his own story of childhood abuse and pain and how it contributed to anger issues and relationship difficulties in his home and ministry. He then continued sharing the solution. "Most of us have heard how Jesus bore our sins on the cross, but we rarely hear how he also bore our emotional pain from the sins committed against us. Here it is in Isaiah chapter 53 along with a promise of healing:

> 'Surely he took up our pain
> and bore our suffering,
> yet we considered him punished by God,
> stricken by him, and afflicted.
> But he was pierced for our transgressions,
> he was crushed for our iniquities;
> the punishment that brought us peace was on him,
> and by his wounds we are healed.
> We all, like sheep, have gone astray,
> each of us has turned to our own way;
> and the Lord has laid on him
> the iniquity of us all.'"

After sharing their stories, Clair and Clara would give an appeal that went like this: "Brothers and sisters, after you have told your painful stories, and after you have identified your lies and vows, and after you have wept the tears that have been there all along, you can pray and release all of that to Jesus on the cross. Some find writing effective. Write out what happened to you. Write down the feelings the experience gave you, and your lies and vows. Later, when you are in your counseling session, read the letter out loud, let the tears flow, and pray. At the end of the week, we will all go outside, make a fire, and burn those letters. It will be a time you'll remember: 'This is the day I let all that go.'"

Dr. Clair called this process – Talk – Pray – Be Healed. He based it on James 5:16, which says, "Confess your faults one to another, and pray one for another, that ye may be healed."

As the years went on and I was leading many courses myself, I had the students nail those letters onto a wooden cross we had set up in the classroom, identifying where the old self really was "crucified with Christ" (Galatians 2:20). Then, after burning the letters on the last day of the course we'd go inside. Each student would then be surrounded by classmates who would speak out Bible verses concerning their new identity in Christ.

The course presented basic truths using various models, illustrations, and activities that would resonate with students uniquely. I marveled how Clair and Clara modeled this way of presenting, all the while trusting the Holy Spirit and being true to proven principles.

I was so thankful for the success of the workshops, but as we flew back to Sisimiut, I began to realize the toll that the Greenland work was taking on our family. *How many times had we been through this now!* Joyce and the kids had not only been back and forth with me to Greenland, but they had moved from town to town across the country.

I didn't have to ponder and pray about this one long—it was clear we should take advantage of the opportunity to return to Canada with Clair and Clara the very next day.

It was -54 degrees Celsius when we arrived in Iqaluit. As cold as it was, there was no running straight into the terminal to warm up. The Cheyenne had to be put to bed. This time the engine heater would be plugged in for sure. We arrived safely at the Northern Youth Programs (NYP) hangar the next day. But before we drove home, Clair and Clara invited our family to stay with them for two days. They knew our family had some pain in the heart too, and they opened their home and their hearts to us.

* * *

Walking into their wilderness home, a giant moose head on the wall made it seem we were in a great hunting lodge. The room was filled with many artifacts that were gifts from First Nations and Inuit people in appreciation for their ministry—each with a story attached.

Those days turned out to be a fun private-wilderness-family-counseling-retreat with the founders of the NYP mission themselves. This simple living, servant-hearted couple radiated warmth and hope in one of the world's coldest and most challenging environments.

Clair asked me to preach in their NYP church on Sunday morning. My message, titled *Four Stages to Reaching a Nation,* was originally from a simple printout I'd received from YWAM International. By this time, I had made it my own ministry guide. Here are the main points:

TARGET – Start with prayer for the people group on your heart; They could be a school, a city, your neighbours, or a whole nation. Do research. Pray for workers (Luke 6:2).

ENGAGE – "GO"and meet them. Eat their food. Find "a man of peace" to partner with. Bring healing (see Luke 10:3–9).

PIONEER – The discipleship stage of pioneering has to do with helping establish believers in their faith and seeing them formed into healthy gospel fellowships (churches). Pioneering can also be done through planting a ministry center, like a Youth With A Mission base, from which to launch discipleship, healing, and outreach ministries.

REACHED – Missiologists describe a nation as "reached" when 20 percent are believers, and the unreached have easy access to the gospel in their area. Stir up in the "reached" a desire to do outreach to others of their own culture, and the "called out ones" to other unreached people groups.

I told the NYP church about my experiences in Greenland. "Since those early days I've had the privilege to observe change little by little until the great surge of openness took off with the Jesus Film outreach and the Pain of the Heart ministry. I believe there is much more to come."

As it turned out, the surge of openness seen during these outreaches would simply be a taste of what we would witness on our next trip to Greenland. What happened next was so powerful that it was like a continuation of the Book of Acts. It was an event that would be indelibly recorded in our minds and hearts for the rest of our lives. The Pain of the Heart ministry would be there like a perfectly placed fishing net.

One of our earliest one-week Biblical Counseling courses in 2002 with Dr. Clair Schnupp teaching and Brian Wind translating. In 2013 Brian accepted the challenge of overseeing the ministry in Greenland.

Chapter 18

A Turning Point in History

A few weeks later I visited the Mission House in Nuuk on my way back to Sisimiut for a counseling course and the annual INO conference. I had barely gotten through the door when my pastor friend John Østergaard greeted me with joy.

"Errol, it's amazing what has been happening here. The first night of our Easter healing meetings we had to turn 150 people away. People just kept coming and coming. We've never seen anything like it."

"John, that's wonderful. Tell me more."

"The people were so attentive and respectful in the meetings. Two blind people received their sight, two deaf received hearing, people lined up and waited patiently for hours to be prayed for. There were many miracles. And we've had only positive coverage on TV news and radio."

I felt a rush of joy at hearing about this move of God among the people I loved.

John continued: "Danish evangelists Hans and Inge Bernsten have been preaching. They said, 'If this is what Jesus can do for your body, just think what he can do in your heart.' And many have received Christ as their savior."

That afternoon I also visited Lars Peter, who happened to be in Nuuk at the time. He said, "I'm going out to help a friend prepare some seal meat. Do you want to come with me?" After my long trip from Kelowna it was refreshing to be in the open air by the harbor watching the two men skillfully work. For fun, they tossed pieces of seal fat to hovering seagulls. The birds fought for each morsel in midair as if in a rugby scrum. Preparing the seal meat took about an hour in a bent-over position. In the car driving back Lars Peter said, "My friend used to have a lot of back pain after a job like that but he was healed in the Easter meetings."

There was still so much need for healing in this land. When I reached Sisimuit a call was waiting for me. It was from one of our former DTS students, a member of the Zionsborg fellowship. "A woman in town wants us to come and pray for her. Can you come with us, Eroli?"

"*Suu, ilaana, aggilersanga*—Yes, of course, I'm coming."

We were welcomed into the weathered, wood frame house of a grandmother whose dark eyes welled with pain. She began to cry, "It's been so hard. I don't have strength anymore. My daughter's husband committed suicide and the son feels like his presence is here. We have had healers come and talk to us, but when they leave there are more spirits. We want them to leave. We hear noises at night."

It blessed me to observe my friend take leadership in ministering to this woman. Joined by another former DTS student from town, we prayed earnestly through the house.

My next ministry opportunity was as troubling as the first. I was asked to help dig a grave for a woman who had been beaten to death by her own son. The mother's name was Juaanna. Joyce and I had visited her a few months earlier at the request of her daughter. Juaanna struggled with alcoholism and depression. When we prayed for her, the troubled woman brightened. She said, "I feel a peace and warmth has come over me."

Sadly, the gospel of peace had not yet reached her son. He should have been helping dig his mother's grave, for in Greenland the family is responsible for burying their loved ones. But he was now in jail.

A few days later, we began the Biblical Counselors Training Course with twenty-two students. Most suffered from "big A" abuse experiences. The first day of the course started out with a full roll of tissue for every three people at a table. By the end of the week, every roll was used up, soaked with tears of anguish. Dr. Clair said, "More pain has come up so far in Greenland than in any other place we've been with the workshop."

The proud and unbelieving can't be set free. Like Jesus said to the Pharisees, "You will die in your sins." God won't twist anybody's arm to accept Him, but he always has His arms open and ready to comfort, heal, deliver, save, and prosper those who will believe. That's exactly what hundreds of Greenlandic people were doing during these remarkable days, which turned into remarkable years.

Following the workshop, I began setting up for the INO conference. John called from Nuuk, "Errol, why don't we hold some open public meetings during the conference days. Perhaps we'll see great things happen like we did in Nuuk at Easter."

After praying with a small DTS team who'd come up from Alaska for their outreach I booked the town hall for two nights. Just 24 hours before the first meeting was to begin, we put up posters around town. That's all that was needed. Many had heard about what happened in Nuuk, and by meeting time the hall was overflowing.

We'd set up 150 chairs, but people were standing together wall to wall, a crowd nearing 400. Many people responded to the gospel message that night. Hundreds received prayer for every kind of sickness and bondage.

The same thing happened the next evening. As the crowds kept coming a man came over to me, "We can't let any more people in, it is getting dangerous," he said.

Another woman I'd never seen before came over and said, "You should have had the meetings in the sports hall, which is much bigger. There is so much need." If only we'd thought of that earlier, but thankfully God was bigger than the building.

At one point during that second evening I was standing onstage observing the sea of faces. It was like a dream. I was filled with awe and joy and holy fear at the sight of so many spiritually hungry faces. More than once I asked myself, *Is this really happening?* Seeing the tightly packed crowd waiting patiently for individual prayer was like looking at a huge tree heavy-laden with overripe fruit—such longing and desperation for God's help.

I watched the ministry team from Nuuk, who had been involved in the Easter meetings, praying for people one after the other at several prayer stations. Suddenly, faith and desire welled up inside of me. *I have to get down there and help pray for the people!* Then I saw one of the Greenlandic believers nearby and I asked, "Will you pray with me for the people?"

Just before motioning the first person over for prayer, I looked at my watch. It was 9:30 p.m. Earlier, I noticed the prayer team declare short, one-sentence prayers of faith over the people, and there had been results. So that's what I did.

We prayed for one young man who had a bad back and legs. Afterward I asked, "How do you feel now?" Breaking into a big smile, and twisting from side to side, he said, "There is no more pain."

"What do you want prayer for?" I asked one teenage girl.

"Please pray for my eyes." So we did.

"How are you now?"

She broke into tears. "I can see colors!"

Another woman told us, "I have pain in my stomach and eczema all over my body."

When we prayed, she too burst into tears. "I feel the power of God all over me!"

There was the desperate young mother with an uncontrollable child, a daughter with a mother at home dying of cancer, and on and on it went. Such need, such anguish, such desperation, meeting divine-healing-grace.

The next time I looked up over the crowd, there were only a few left in line. When I glanced at my watch again, it was 11:30 p.m. We'd been praying for two hours steady, and the others had been going longer than that. It's hard to find the words to describe what we witnessed during those two special days. People started streaming into Zionsborg during the day, some asking for Bibles, and others for prayer. Similar stories were being reported from all over town. Many who attended those meetings still are following Jesus today.

One day a couple came into the Zionsborg meeting room as I was standing there. The man, who I'd never seen before, asked, "Can you show me and my wife how to become Christians?"

I was stunned. During the eighteen years I'd served in Greenland, we'd gone out many times to share the gospel. Never had people come to us asking how to receive Christ. It was clearly a move of the Holy Spirit.

I told the couple at Zionsborg, "I'm on my way out right now, but my friend here would love to tell you." I motioned to a young woman nearby who was tuning her guitar. She looked a little surprised, but she jumped up to meet them. That day the couple received Christ and sang with the choir in a big meeting that very night. Both later took the Pain of the Heart course and became part of the Zionsborg fellowship.

On the last day of the INO conference in Zionsborg I noticed an impressive looking Greenlandic man come in the door to the meeting room.

David Åsblom told me later, "That man you saw is a worker at the power plant that I oversee. He is also an influential person in town—he sits on the town council. This morning he was having coffee with the other workers. One of the men said, 'My son's ear was healed in the meeting last night.' In response he said, 'I'm going up to Zionsborg right now to get my leg prayed for.' He did, and he was healed."

David continued, "When this man came back to work, he said to me, 'I think I am going to believe in this way. And how long has Zionsborg been reaching out to people? As a town we should do something to support it.' "

David, who'd lived in Sisimiut all his life, then declared with awe, "I have never witnessed anything like what's been happening in town this week. I feel like I am standing on some key point of history." Yes, it truly felt like a turning point for the gospel in Greenland. An unforgettable time for all who were there.

David's excitement reminded me of another incredible spiritual breakthrough. In Acts 2 Peter is preaching to a very large crowd, "Repent and be baptized every one of you in the name of Jesus Christ for the remission of sins, and ye shall receive the gift of the Holy Ghost. For the promise is unto you, and to your children, and to all that are afar off...Then they that gladly received his word were baptized, and the same day were added unto them about three thousand souls. And they continued steadfastly in the apostles' doctrine and fellowship, and in breaking of bread, and in prayers..."

That took place 2000 years ago, and similar responses are still happening all over the world as believers share the life-changing message of the gospel (Matthew 28:19–20). The Greenlandic believers were on fire for God during those days. With joy and love they sought fellowship together in the Lord, offered warm hospitality, and in power ministered to others.

Another awakening was simultaneously happening in a place with a similar climate and culture. It was from this region that God stirred the hearts of two pastors who would come with their team and spread more of the glory with their long-lost cousins.

Breakthrough, spiritual awakening, and revival was happening in Sisimiut!

Chapter 19

Long-Lost Cousins

The Pain of the Heart workshops touched a need so deep it was like triggering a spiritual tsunami across Greenland. After every workshop we heard encouraging testimonies like the one from 30-year-old Aviaq.

"When I first came into class, I didn't believe there was a God who could help me. My parents were alcoholics and I became an alcoholic drug addict. I had been sexually abused, and I became an abuser of others. But now I'm getting the stones and hardness out. During these days you uncovered many hurts, and they have been healed. If you had not come here my life would still be full of lies and anger. I now believe in a God who cares."

In Greenland, there often would be a high dropout rate in an intensive six-day course like this—not because the programs were poor but because students struggling with addictions or dysfunctional home life found it hard to concentrate. But they didn't drop out of these workshops. The teaching dealt head-on with these issues and everyone was desperate for help.

That same year, God brought more encouragement from an unexpected direction—the Inuit churches of Eastern Canada. James Taqaugaq (Arreak) from Iqaluit, Nunavut, and Billy Arnaquq from Qikiqtarjuaq, Nunavut, asked to come and minister in the churches of Greenland. Both are Inuit pastors who had been featured on the popular Transformation II documentary, "The Glory Spreads." The film revealed the plight of many Arctic communities in Canada and told how widespread spiritual renewal had resulted in the burning of thousands of dollars worth of pornographic materials, drugs, and other enslaving materials.

Through tears, the interviewees expressed pain over the brokenness in their communities. One said, "It was terrible, so much drunkenness, so much abuse, so many suicides. It was an awful time." And then with overwhelming tears of gratefulness, "We are so thankful for the Lord's visitation among us. We now have hope in Jesus."

James and Billy were part of this awakening and wanted to share the glory in Greenland. "Errol, could you set up a one-week evangelistic outreach for our team?" Billy asked.

"Yes!" I began making arrangements immediately.

On a brutally cold morning in November 26, 2002, I joined their team on a chartered Air Nunavut plane that took off in a cloud of snow from the Iqaluit airport. Interestingly, it was exactly 20 years earlier to the day that I'd received the word *Greenland* in my prayer time. I could never have imagined all that would transpire from acting on that one word impression.

Our first meeting was in Maniitsoq and the townspeople came out in droves. Not only because of the new climate of openness but because they wanted to meet their "long-lost Inuit cousins" from Arctic Canada. They had plenty of laughs listening to each other talk in their own dialects. For example, in Kalaallisut (Greenlandic) *paasivarit* means "I understand you," but in Eastern Arctic Inuktitut it means "I'm going to wrestle (with) you."

That evening James gave a clear gospel message in English with Brian interpreting. Earlier in the day, one of the elders had said to us, "I know what happened in Nuuk and I know what happened in Sisimiut at the INO conference, but I can hardly believe it will happen here. I know the people!"

But the miracles continued. The old Lutheran State Church building used for the meeting was full to overflowing. Most people who came forward for prayer said, "Yes, I want Jesus in my life." Prayer stations were set up around the building with two ministers at each spot ready to talk and pray with anyone who wanted it.

About twenty people, including a group of teenage girls, lined up to talk and pray with me and a prayer partner. Some literally fell into our arms weeping. We heard the familiar stories of living in an alcoholic home. Most were suicidal. One of the girls said, "I just want to be loved." Two of the others said, "Before tonight I did not know God existed, but now I know He does."

After two evening meetings in Maniitsoq plus sessions with church leaders, we left on a ship for Sisimiut. The first two hours on board were pleasant, and one of the team remarked, "This is going to be like heaven with the beautiful scenery." But once we hit open water, the daylong voyage felt nothing like heaven. Winter winds and raging waves thrashed the ship as it crossed the Arctic Circle. Most of the team became seasick and one said, "I feel like I'm dying!" Billy, who'd worked on ships before, kept running around saying, "The answer is to keep moving." But the others were too far gone by then—laying pale and groaning upon their bunks with little white bags ready. Later Billy said, "I've never seen so many sick people in my life!"

We arrived in Sisimiut a little woozy, two hours late for our scheduled meeting, but an enthusiastic crowd was still waiting for us. We soon revived, excited to find people who were so receptive. Day after day they came to the meetings and many new ones opened their hearts to Jesus.

After four nights of meetings in Sisimiut we were ready to move on. I was in the kitchen of the Zionsborg Mission House preparing breakfast when the phone rang. It was the pilot for Air Nunavut calling from Iqaluit. "The airport in Sisimiut won't let us land today because of strong winds, so we'll have to try again tomorrow." When the people in town heard we'd be there one more day they called another meeting for that evening. Again, a large crowd showed up, and many reached out for spiritual help.

One woman I counseled that night had come forward with her husband. After praying to receive Jesus, she said, "Now I feel so different in my heart."

I asked, "Is there anything else you want prayer for? God wants you to know he is here and you can trust Him."

She opened up about that awful subject—sexual abuse. Two female believers joined me in the office, together with this woman, to talk more. She told us:

"About five years ago a memory came up of being abused as a four year old. I couldn't remember who it was who did this, but my life sunk into darkness with that memory. It's like I became paralyzed. The doctor gave me morphine shots, and I told my husband to leave me. I said, 'You can't live with a woman like me.' But my husband comforted me and stood with me."

I told her what I'd heard Dr. Clair say, "God never intended for this to happen to you. This person listened to the voice of the devil (or their own sinful nature), but God was saying, "Don't do it!"

I've heard some Christians say, "God let this happen to you because He knew you could handle it." That misguided statement is contrary to the character of God, the commandments of the Bible, and everything Jesus modeled and taught in the New Testament. Like so many others, this woman blamed God for what happened.

"I've been so angry with God and I have spoken bad to Him," she said.

After receiving God's forgiveness and extending forgiveness to her abuser she said,

"My husband keeps asking, 'What do you want for your birthday?' I said, 'Nothing. I don't desire anything.' Finally, I said, 'I want a Bible.' He bought that for me."

"That's good, because you need to read it and understand how much God loves you. You also need to confront the lies you believed about yourself and God because of the abuse you experienced."

After acknowledging where the lies came from, and how destructive they had been in her life, she prayed and let them go.

"That destructive identity died with Jesus on the cross. You are now risen with Christ, by faith, into a new identity, a new self in Jesus. You are a highly valued member of his family."

Her face lit up with joy.

* * *

The year 2002 was amazing, and the fresh wind of healing grace wasn't slowing down. Over the next decade there were more Arctic flights, counseling courses, changed lives, and unexpected ministry opportunities. In that span, fifty-eight students completed our nine-week, in-depth courses. Another 500 took our one-week courses in sixteen of the largest towns in Greenland. In 2013, Greenlander Brian Wind was commissioned into full-time work with the Pain of the Heart ministry. This had long been our dream—that native Greenlanders would carry on the training in their own language. And now that was happening.

One of the many highlights for me during those years of ministry with Clair and Clara was flying into Qaanaaq (population 600) to meet the most northern indigenous people in the world. We were hosted by Arqiunguaq and Tukummeq Qaerngaaq, a gracious and joyful couple who had come to Jesus a few years earlier through the ministry of Greenlandic believers from farther south down the coast. Tukummeq told me one day, "We used to be nothing. We were drunks and so low. We were bad parents. Oh, I'm so glad for my new life. We love Jesus." They were passing this love to others in town. By now scores had come to the Lord through their testimony and were attending the meetings in their home.

This amazing couple both attended our one-week course and were able to process deep traumas from their past. They later graduated from our longer counseling course in Nuuk, and have helped many others since.

We visited Qaanaaq for the first time in January, and all day it was pitch dark except for a faint orange glow on the south horizon. The town had a few streetlights, and it was so dark we had no idea what the town looked like until we returned the following September.

Like his ancestors, Arqiunguaq hunted for food and income. Qaanaaq has more full-time hunters than any other region in Greenland. Arqiunguaq's work was fraught with danger and he told his most remarkable story as we were sitting around a table, during the 2015 INO conference in Sisimiut.

"I was out hunting *nanok* (polar bears) when my sled dogs surrounded one. In the commotion, the *nanok* slashed one of my precious dogs in the eye. I prayed to Jesus on my way back to Qaanaaq. I felt so bad about the dog's injury. When we arrived, I secured my dogs and went into town. A midwife heard me telling the story and asked if she and a doctor could help. The doctor, with his knife, took the bad eye out and threw it on the snow. Five of us were watching." Galya, an arctic photographer, was not only watching, but took pictures during the operation. A few days later she took pictures of the dog again because something amazing had happened.[5]

Aqiunnguaq explained, "After two days we went and looked at iPhone, that's the name of the dog. I could see it was looking at me with two eyes! I got startled; could it really be true? The dog was acting happy, as if he was showing off his two eyes to us. After this experience my faith in God got bigger and my doubts got smaller."

Arqiunguaq and Tukummeq later repeated this story on film for my son Anthony and fellow filmmaker Sam McLoughlin. As they retold the story, tears rolled down their cheeks—not tears of sadness, but tears of joy reflecting the goodness of God. With the eye healing story, we can surely say God's healing work in Greenland went way beyond expectations (see Ephesians 3:20–21).

While we were in Qaanaaq, Clair and I had discussed the possibility of traveling to Siorapaluk, which was said to be the world's northernmost native settlement. The ancestors of its residents arrived there generations ago. We were told it would be a five-hour dog sled trip to get there. Because we were so busy with the course in Qaanaaq, and because we were told the sea ice was dangerous for traveling, we didn't go. However, upon leaving Qaanaaq Dr. Clair aimed the airplane north

5 A special thanks to Galya Morrell, an arctic ice-artist and explorer, for her generosity in sharing with me her before and after pictures of iPhone's eye, and her own testimony of the event.

before going south and circled the small village. In the pitch dark I could see its lights below and prayed for the people. While in Qaanaaq, we prayed with a young couple from Siorapaluk who had not attended our course. What a privilege. Jesus said, "But ye shall receive power, after that the Holy Ghost is come upon you: and ye shall be witnesses unto me both in Jerusalem, and in all Judaea, and in Samaria, and unto the uttermost part of the earth." I guess we could safely say this couple represented those from the uttermost part of the earth!

There are so many wonderful stories from every one of the sixteen towns we visited during those years. In between the Greenland trips, I was involved with the course in other places too: some together with Clair and Clara's team, some with others in the counseling ministry, and some by myself. Several times I taught the course at the University of the Nations in Kona, Hawaii.

A couple of years after facilitating the course in Kona, at the Foundations Counseling Ministry School, I attended an International YWAM conference in Kansas City. As I waited in line for coffee one day, a woman behind me said, "Please let me buy your coffee. When you were teaching in Kona, I received a big breakthrough in my life!" Many similar testimonies throughout the years showed the course was not just head knowledge but an experience at the heart level with Jesus. Through his death, burial, and resurrection, Jesus opened the way for all to be set free.

Most professing Christians have invited Christ to be their savior. Few have had the opportunity to be guided through the process of putting off the old self with its wounds and putting on the new self through "the grace of God in all its truth," (Colossians 1:6 NIV; Ephesians 4:22-24). To my great astonishment, I found that I had not fully grasped "the grace of God in all its truth." This revelation soon took me to a place of deliverance and freedom I desperately needed.

Removing the wounded eye

iPhone with a new eye!

Chapter 20

My Great Discovery

Working with Clair and Clara gave me fresh confidence to teach what I had learned from them. I led one-on-one counseling sessions, did staff training in skill development, taught some of the Biblical counselors training course material, and gradually expanded out on my own in Canada, Europe, and the United States. Early on they invited me to present one of the counseling models and to weave my own testimony into it. The model I chose was "The Shame Circle."

I saw the power of this theme one evening when I was ministering on Vancouver Island, BC, to a group of teenagers in Ucluelet. The boys were playing floor hockey when I arrived with our team. The youth leader came over and said, "I don't think we should even bother trying to talk to these teens tonight. They are worked up and just won't listen."

I decided to go ahead and speak to them for a few minutes. I shared the story of when I was attacked by a gang of boys who pelted me with dirt clods and how that experience, along with many others of similar nature, contributed to my feelings of shame, contempt, and destructive heart beliefs.

As I shared, the teens became dead quiet, so I went on and finished by saying,

"At age sixteen, I began bodybuilding and got new confidence. For the first time in years, I felt good about myself, and was getting some compliments. However, even though I got some joy and affirmation from the weight training, I still felt empty and restless inside. That's when I cried out to God. And he touched me. I experienced a deep heart transformation through making Jesus Lord of my life. My relationship with God has given me a sense of purpose I could never have imagined."

The teens listened intently to the end, and it was clear they were touched by the message. Pain of the heart can be found everywhere, and addressing it openly has proven to be a powerful ministry approach. Clair described it as "entering people's lives through their pain." It even works with rowdy teens.

But there was something important missing from my story—a stunning truth which I still hadn't seen. The Apostle Paul addresses it in his epistles. It's a truth that will set you free if you grasp it. Most serious-minded Christians accept it as a foundational doctrine but haven't lived it. That was my experience. I knew the verses. I preached it. I experienced it in my life to a degree, and yet I was still blind. One morning not long afterward, around the year 2010, I watched a Christian TV program while eating breakfast. The host interviewed a Bible teacher who shook me to the core with his responses. He said, "The church in general simply does not believe in the death, burial, and resurrection of Jesus Christ. By their lifestyle, Christians deny it."

I thought to myself, *What committed believer would ever deny that!*

Then he turned to the camera and said, "If you are doing anything at all to earn God's blessings, you are denying the death, burial, and resurrection of Jesus."

His over-the-top way of expressing this set me on a soul searching journey. I came to realize this was true of me! I tried to keep the commandments, confess my flaws, struggle for victory, and pray—all for the purpose of presenting myself acceptable before God. Yet I never felt quite good enough, victorious enough, or acceptable enough. I couldn't just rest in God's love.

The Apostle Paul rebuked the church in Galatia for this very thing. He said, "Are ye so foolish? Having begun in the Spirit, are ye now made perfect by the flesh?" (Galatians 3:3). In my times of heart preparation, I'd been asking God to do what he had already done. He had already provided everything through the death, burial, and resurrection of his son Jesus Christ. My old self was buried with Jesus, and my new self has risen with Jesus, period.

God had already delivered me from the need to fix myself, because you can't fix a dead man. He'd already delivered me from the need to make myself more holy, because you can't get more holy than the Spirit of Christ in you. I finally chose to believe this, rejoice in this, and see myself as a friend of God.

Paul described this transition so well in Colossians 1:21–23: "And you, that were sometime alienated and enemies in your mind by wicked works, yet now hath he reconciled (made friends). In the body of his (Jesus') flesh through death, to present you holy and unblameable and unreproveable in his sight: If ye continue in the faith grounded and settled, and be not moved away from the hope of the gospel, which ye have heard…"

Notice it says we are presented holy, unblameable, and unreprovable in God's sight as we continue believing it's all in Jesus. I don't ever want to move away from this hope. I don't ever want to slip back under the law in trying to gain God's approval through my own efforts.

I fully embraced this new approach to God on a warm summer day as I sat in our backyard shed looking out to the garden. For a moment, I watched a hummingbird flutter along to suck nectar out of the flowers. I then closed my eyes and imagined meeting God in the secret place of my heart. Instead of asking if there was any sin in my life I needed to deal with, I came before him thanking him, by faith, for the clean heart he gave me in Jesus. I felt full acceptance in his love because I knew he saw in me the righteousness of Jesus. His love transformed my heart. My first love for God returned and new blessings flowed in my life.

One immediate change was a renewed love for Joyce. Part of this change had to do with my subconscious dependence on my dear wife.

I had looked to her for a depth of love, acceptance, and approval that can only come from God. If we look to others instead of him, we will become disappointed and angry at the very people we are supposed to love, lead, and protect. At the same time, we'll be a disappointment to them because we are not leading and living from a place of strength, security, and joy.

Though we may have God-given ability to lead ministries and help others come to faith, our weaknesses always show up in our closest relationships. Tensions in our homes and workplaces can escalate to a point that they harm the people closest to us and undermine the ministry outcomes we work so hard to achieve. Our tendency as humans is to change the people around us so we feel more successful and peaceful. However, if we do not make them feel honored and cherished, our efforts to change them will have the opposite effect.

I've been blessed many times by praying, "Thank you, Lord, that I am crucified with Christ (Galatians 2:20). Thank you that all the shame, anger, lust, pride, fear, and worry is buried. Thank you, Lord, that in Jesus my old self does not exist."

Many believers would say, "What do you mean it doesn't exist? We struggle with our human weakness every day!" Well, the Bible says the old man is dead to the believer. I've decided to accept that and get rid of thoughts, emotions, words, and actions that are not in harmony with my new self. This sounds like a contradiction, but it's not. While negative emotions and beliefs may linger in the brain and emotional memories of our bodies, they are not in our new self. "Do not conform to the pattern of this world, but be transformed by the renewing of your mind." (Romans 12:2). It doesn't say, "try to renew your old self with its habit patterns and vices," but it says, "be transformed by the renewing of your mind." In other words, renew how you see and think about yourself. Your new self in Christ cannot be polluted because Christ can't be polluted. See your new self in Christ as untouchable by this sinful world. "Therefore, if any man be in Christ, he is a new creature: old things are passed away; behold, all things are become new" (2 Corinthians 5:17).

In the Pain of the Heart workshops, we help people expose, confess, and be set free from negative emotional memories and beliefs. But even as we were going through the process of putting off all that pain and darkness, *the new self was still intact.* At the same time, some were born again (received their new self) for the first time as they were releasing the darkness, and thanking God for the peace and healing they were now receiving through what Jesus Christ had done for them on the cross (Isaiah 53:5).

* * *

I still love to sit alone in the early morning. I cover my eyes, relax my breathing, and approach the Throne of Grace in the secret place of my heart. Then I meditate on the Scriptures. The negative emotions and beliefs that dominated my childhood are now a distant memory. In the secret place of my heart new emotions of love, gratitude, and praise spring forth daily. These times before the Throne of Grace are continuing to establish my identity in Christ, and releasing more fruits of the Spirit.

On one of the flights to Greenland with the Schnupps, Dr. Clair told me about the new autopilot he had installed in the Cheyenne. "Errol, this is an amazing device. I can set it to any airport in North America, Mexico, or Greenland and the airplane will take me directly there."

The heart of a human being is kind of like that autopilot. Once it's set, our lives often go in that direction. Tragically, traumatic experiences of childhood program the autopilot of many hearts. But praise God, we can not only change course, we can receive a brand-new autopilot system—a new heart. As God promised in Ezekiel 36:26, "I will give you a new heart and put a new spirit in you; I will remove from you your heart of stone and give you a heart of flesh."

Many in the world are, in their minds, sitting in a prison of dark hopelessness. They can't see that the prison door is wide open. Jesus has opened the door through his resurrection. I am so thankful to all those who have stepped out in faith to bring me a message from God's Word. Those timely words helped set me free and grow in my walk with God. I'm also thankful to all I've had the privilege of partnering with for God's Kingdom work in various parts of the world, especially Greenland, and especially with the wonderful Greenlandic people.

Ever since I had my eyes opened to this more complete understanding of what God has given in Jesus, I can't stop talking about it. It *is* the gospel. I believe it is the central message of the *good news* that Jesus commanded us to preach in all the world (along with the great importance of discipleship, Matthew 28:19–20). Today the world needs millions more to experience it, to live it, and to teach it. Will you be one of them?

Epilogue

When the Schnupps and our team finished our last Pain of the Heart course in Greenland in 2013, I thought I was just getting started. Over the next year, the courses took me to many places outside of Greenland. I was seeing wonderful results in people's lives and was full of vision for the ministry. But then suddenly and shockingly, after 12 amazing years, that ministry came to a screeching halt.

My approach to counseling had been profoundly influenced by my renewed understanding of what the Apostle Paul describes as "the grace of God in all its truth" (as I shared in chapter 20). Because of this I began to edge the course in a slightly different direction that my dear friend and mentor, Dr. Clair, was not comfortable with. We had some long conversations about this and eventually he said, "I now understand where you are coming from and I feel much better about it."

Nevertheless, one Saturday morning in June 2014 I felt certain I was to resign from that ministry, at least for the time being. This meant letting go of my goals to complete a master's degree in counseling and to take Pain of the Heart training far and wide in YWAM. Not long after however, four new visions appeared in plain sight, bringing Greenland back as my primary ministry focus:

New Vision for Greenland Tour

In recognition of YWAM Greenland's 30th anniversary, I launched a tour of Western Canada for the purpose of bringing encouragement to supporters through the Greenland story, which I presented in a PowerPoint presentation. The tour also raised funds for a second vision.

Greenland Story Documentary

This turned out to be an amazing experience. I got to work with my son Anthony and his filmmaker friend Sam McLoughlin, who agreed to join me in Greenland. There they captured twenty inspiring stories revealing transformed lives in that nation. Subsequently, Arnannguaq Thiessen, a dear Greenlandic friend of our family, translated many of these testimonies into English. Afterward, I had these great stories but no idea how to make a documentary. It was then that I received an unexpected phone call from a young man, Felix Gover, the director of a Holland-based Christian film company called Living Image. He said, "We want to make a documentary in Greenland. Can you help us?" Imagine the significance and timing of that call!

I replied to Felix, "Believe it or not, I'm trying to make a documentary on Greenland right now." Felix proposed we work together and I heartily agreed. The result was a powerful, award-winning, 28-minute documentary on the transformed life of Lars Peter Jensen called *Arctic Light*. It is a wonderful tool for the gospel, set amidst the stunning scenery of Greenland. The documentary is available to watch in Greenlandic, Danish, and English. (See more information below)

Reaching the Lost Youth of Greenland

My Canadian friend, Dr. Alfred Laskowski, had been running summer Wilderness Youth Outreach and Training in Greenland, under YWAM Greenland, for years. Out of this program two young men became especially enthused about this ministry. Alfred felt it was now time to initiate another level of training, and it was time for me to help. We ran two youth leadership training courses in Nuuk, together with another youth wilderness ministry founded by Dr. Ashley Denton, author of Christian Outdoor Leadership. The seeds from these courses are in germination stage and we are believing God for much fruit through the Greenlandic youth of this generation.

Write a Book on the Greenland Story

You are holding it in your hands right now, thanks to a lot of help from others. During the last half of this writing journey, I was at the same time caring for my elderly father as he suffered through the stages of cancer. This led to another new experience as his personal representative once he breathed his last. During much of this time we were all experiencing the pandemic. Because of caring for my father, and because of the pandemic, I stopped traveling for a season. What better project could there have been than writing a book.

See the Bible Translated into North and East Greenlandic

This vision is in process, and I am involved along with Wycliff Bible Translators, and others, including a number of enthused North and East Greenlanders! www.endbiblepovertynow.com.

The next ministry chapter

Even though I am now 70 years old, I'm still in Youth With A Mission and I still have vision. I trust you have vision too. Go for it dear reader.

Family

After moving back to Canada as a family in 1996, **Joyce** began her Masters' degree in TESOL, serving in that profession ever since.

Our four grown children now lead full lives of their own in serving professions.

Tanya is married with two girls and serves skillfully in the health care profession. She and her husband Tristan enjoy involvement with their local church. **Jayna** is married with two girls and a boy, presently serving in the Media School at the YWAM University of the Nations campus in Kona, Hawaii. Her husband Jono serves the campus through his skills as a water engineer. **Angela** is a skilled midwife. In her times off she loves hiking with her beautiful Lassie dog. **Anthony** is a graphic designer and co-owner of Cool Hand Print Co. He is also a song writer/musician with his band ICELANDIA. Bouldering and surfing are his favorite recreations. In spite of a few hardships, each one of our children say they wouldn't trade their mission lives in Greenland.

Greenland

Brian Wind

After Brian had been commissioned into full-time ministry with the biblical counseling ministry in 2013, it wasn't long before I received word that he had run a one week course in Sisimiut with 40 students!

Just as exciting was all the help Brian had for the one-on-one caregiving sessions, because many of the local believers were now trained to do it, and everything could be done in their mother tongue, with no need for interpretation. Brian has run many courses since his commissioning, and also serves in an elder capacity for Inuunerup Nutaap Oqaluffia (New Life Church). Angaju, Brian's wife, who also attended DTS with him in 1989, has remained a faithful wife, mother and servant in the church.

Sven-Olov Åsblom continues a life of service to the less fortunate, and to the INO church in Greenland. His father Rune, who pioneered the mission in Sisimiut decades ago (along with his wife Gunvor and family), recently passed away.

Lars Peter and Bolette Jensen are presently living in Denmark having better access to health care for their grandson, Pituaq (who appears in the documentary Arctic Light). Shortly after filming it was discovered Pituaq had leukemia. Today, however, he is well. Lars Peter said, "My main purpose in life is to help others." He continues to do that in Denmark, which is home to more than 16,000 Greenlanders. Bolette works in a government office, and has always served alongside her husband.

Dr. Clair Schnupp and Clara as of this writing, are continuing faithful to their call well into their 80s. After most of their work with Greenland was completed in 2013, they turned their attention back to Canada's Inuit, although they were not able to do as much as they'd hoped because of Covid restrictions. They fly commercially now after piloting themselves for 60 years.

Acknowledgments

To Creator God: "Through you all things were made, and without you nothing was made that has been made" (John 1:3) I declare, "You are Love" (1 John 4:8). Because of who you are, I believe it's fitting to give thanks and honor to you, to obey your righteous commandments, and believe your life-giving promises as found in the Bible.

To all my Greenlandic friends: At first I felt awkward and insecure coming from a different culture and language but I soon came to love your hospitality, your smiles, your laughter, your food, your winters, and your language. I have loved worshipping with you, I have loved observing your humble responses to the Lord. I've loved watching you minister in the power of the Holy Spirit, and I have loved growing together with you in Jesus.

To my dear wife Joyce: When people hear the story of our lives they don't have much compassion for me, but they understandably have a lot for you! You are an amazing woman having taken your first trip across the Arctic Circle on an icebreaker ship, with our 10-day-old-baby girl Angela, our young girls Tanya and Jayna, and then little Anthony the next year. You contributed much to the ministry in Greenland and kept the homefront intact with our four growing children during my frequent ministry travels after we returned to Canada. Through it all, you have been as resolute as iron and as resourceful as a desert spring. You have been the instigator of family fun. You always thrive and make things happen wherever you are, including valuable input for this book. I love you.

To our dear children Tanya, Jayna, Angela and Anthony: You are now mature and prosperous adults. My memories are so full and rich having had the joy of experiencing much of this journey with you in the land of snow. Even as children you were part of the team and blessed many by just being yourselves. I love you all so much.

Thank you to John and Helle Lund, the young couple who first opened the door to me in Nuuk, the capital city of Greenland; to Dan and Gudrun Toldam, who continued to welcome our teams year after year and spoke encouraging words over me; to John and Ulla Østergaard Nielsen, who for three decades embraced our family, our teams, and ministry projects. John's support, skills, hard work, and faith, plus this couples' endless hospitality resulted in much good fruit, including a nationwide Christian radio ministry in partnership with Galcom International.

Gunvor and Rune Åsblom, David and Jeannette Åsblom, Sven-Olov and Kerstin Åsblom: With great generosity you welcomed our family and ministry as partners in the gospel. Zionsborg feels like home.

Sven-Olov: You've been one of God's best gifts to me in Greenland. Through you it was like the floodgates of heaven opened for the ministry I felt called to do. In the early days you seemed like Tarzan, Captain James Cook, and missionary Hudson Taylor all wrapped up in one person. Although we had an amazing partnership in ministry, I'm aware that my cultural ignorance, personal flaws, and constant need for interpretation must have been like a mosquito buzzing in your ear. You'll always be one of my heroes Sven, even though you can't lift me over your head with one hand anymore.

A big shout-out of gratitude to Wayne and Linda Moore, pastors of Iqaluit Pentecostal Church, who never shut the door to our family, our teams, or me whenever a place was needed for the night on the way to and from Greenland. I always enjoyed your fellowship.

Clair and Clara Schnupp: You enriched my life so much, it would take a book to write about it!

Paul Martinson, as a senior YWAM elder and teacher in YWAM Canada, you have been a great friend and encourager from the earliest days of my Greenland experience until today. Paul, you're a rock, and always there to help.

All supporters, intercessors, teachers, encouragers, work teams and YWAM staff: I personally feel deep appreciation for every one of you.

Doug Lockhart: Without you, my friend, this book may never have been written. You're the one who got me to attend the 2017 writing course led by Scott and his wife Sandi in Montana, and the rest is history. Thank you, Doug, for all your words of encouragement and the valuable contribution of your professional writing skills to this manuscript. It helped a lot!

Scott Tompkins: Scott, your offer to edit my book without me even asking was to me as miraculous as almost anything else I've shared in my story. Your generous patience, perseverance, guidance, and encouragement during this six-year project has been to me like a continual updraft under an eagle's wings.

Jayna and Jono Lowe, my dear daughter and son-in-law, you both contributed so much time, skill and value to this work. Thank you!

YWAM Publishing: Thank you, especially Warren Walsh, Tom Bragg, Fred Renich (and others at the ministry) for accepting my manuscript and for all the work you have done to bring this book to its final completion.

Loren Cunningham: Thank you, Loren, for all you have imparted to me personally over the years through your teaching, your vision, your leadership, and our brief encounters from time to time over the years, including the precious time together in Nuuk way back in August of 1986.

Endnotes

Loren Cunningham is the co-founder of Youth With A Mission (YWAM), an ever-expanding global family of ministries born in 1960. Loren is also the co-founder and International Chancellor of YWAM's University of the Nations. Together with his wife, Darlene, Loren's ministry partner from the beginning of YWAM, he currently leads the University of the Nations campus in Kona, Hawaii. Loren has personally traveled to every sovereign nation on earth, all dependent countries, and more than 100 territories and islands for the sake of Christ and the Great Commission. For more see www.ywam.org

Hearing God's Voice

My flip-the-Bible-open story made a deep impression on me as a young man, and truly spoiled me for the ordinary. After all, think of the chances! I received three different verses, each fulfilling two requests while there are only about 55 verses in the whole Bible referencing something about ships in a negative context, and that's out of 32,102 verses!

But, there is more I want to say about this experience; There is a positive side and a negative side. First, I grew in my love for God and his presence, I grew in my trust for him, and I grew in my motivation to ask for his guidance because He can see what we can't see. As I mentioned in the story, *that particular ship never did float the seas as a YWAM ministry (the full story is in Loren's book "Is That Really You God?"), which of course is a pretty strong confirmation to my guidance! The negative outcomes from that amazing experience was that I gradually gave too much dependence on external signs for guidance, rather than nurturing an ear for that "still, small voice" of the Holy Spirit in my heart. Not primarily in the head, but primarily the heart. External signs should normally be seen as secondary confirmations. On the other hand, guidance may come initially through circumstances, but either way there will be a witness in the heart if we have ears to hear. As it says in Colossians 3:15 "Let the peace of God rule in your hearts..." KJV

* Today YWAM has a thriving ship ministry.

Arctic Light Film – Finding Hope in the Darkness

Lars Peter Jensen was born in a small village on the beautiful coast of West Greenland. Sadly, he was raised in a home marred by violence and abuse. Death seemed the only option for his wounded heart until he remembered the gift in his suitcase. This film is in Greenlandic, with English or Danish subtitles

To view the film and find more interesting and helpful information, please visit our website at: www.arcticlightfilm.com

A Word ABout Dialogue Throughout the Book

The dialogue in chapter one was one of the few places throughout the book that I didn't have actual quotes directly from my diaries, or memory. However, the dialogue in chapter one does fit the situation and personalities.

Our young family in Sisimiut
Left to right: Anthony, Angela, Jayna and Tanya in front

Tanya and I during a land break after our struggle through the first of the ice-floes on our way to Narsaq. Those were the very clothes I was wearing when I jumped into the ocean in chapter 9!

A funeral in the graveyard just below Zionsborg, the large yellow building in the background which is a wonderful beachhead for ministry.

An attentive crowd inside the INO church in Maniitsoq during a ministry night with the team representing Arctic Canada. Greenlandic words on the wall from 2 Corinthians 5:17—
Therefore if any man be in Christ, he is a new creature: old things are passed away: behold, all things are become new.

Kings Kids on board the Evangelisten in an ice-free area

Dr. Clair Schnupp, and his wife Clara (L). After taking the course, "How to Handle the Pain of the Heart." Dorthea (R) said, "This week it's like a stone came out of my heart."